Parents Matter

Parents Matter

Supporting Your Child with Math in Grades K–8

Regina M. Mistretta

ROWMAN & LITTLEFIELD
Lanham • Boulder • New York • London

Published by Rowman & Littlefield
A wholly owned subsidiary of The Rowman & Littlefield Publishing Group, Inc.
4501 Forbes Boulevard, Suite 200, Lanham, Maryland 20706
www.rowman.com

Unit A, Whitacre Mews, 26-34 Stannary Street, London SE11 4AB

British Library Cataloguing in Publication Information Available

Library of Congress Cataloging-in-Publication Data Is Available
Names: Mistretta, Regina M., 1965–
Title: Parents matter : supporting your child with math in grades K–8 /
　　Regina M. Mistretta.
Description: Lanham : Rowman & Littlefield, [2016] | Includes bibliographical
　　references.
Identifiers: LCCN 2016029102 (print) | LCCN 2016030537 (ebook) |
　　ISBN 9781475821840 (cloth : alk. paper) | ISBN 9781475821857 (pbk. : alk. paper) |
　　ISBN 9781475821864 (electronic)
Subjects: LCSH: Mathematics—Study and teaching—Parent participation. |
　　Mathematics—Study and teaching (Elementary) | Mathematics—Study and teaching
　　(Middle school) | Education—Parent participation.
Classification: LCC QA135.6 .M56675 2016 (print) | LCC QA135.6 (ebook) | DDC
　　372.7—dc23
LC record available at https://lccn.loc.gov/2016029102

♾ ™ The paper used in this publication meets the minimum requirements of American
National Standard for Information Sciences—Permanence of Paper for Printed Library
Materials, ANSI/NISO Z39.48-1992.

Printed in the United States of America

This book is dedicated:

To my dad, who anchors my efforts to serve as a thoughtful practitioner.

To my former principal, Sister Eileen Mary, for fueling my confidence to innovatively make contributions to schools and families.

And to my dear mentor, Dr. David Fuys, retired professor and chairperson of mathematics education at Brooklyn College, who, to this current day, wisely and patiently guides my professional journey and inspires me to think about thinking.

Contents

Foreword

Parents Matter: Supporting Your Child with Math in Grades K–8 is intended to help parents make sense of the changes in mathematics teaching and learning in Grades kindergarten through 8. Written in an engaging style, this book provides a wonderful resource for parents who want to learn about the current trends in mathematics education and get some ideas about activities they can do with their children.

In chapter 1, the author provides a brief historical account of mathematics education in the United States. As is often the case with historical accounts, this account too is open to different interpretations, which could lead to interesting discussions. The chapter highlights some recurring tensions, such as teaching for meaning and understanding versus teaching for memorization and quick answers, or the tension of teaching as telling versus guiding. As the author explains, it is not an "either-or" situation. An important insight in this chapter is, "Children are encouraged to take risks, and mistakes are viewed as opportunities for learning" (p. 4, ch. 1). Chapter 1 outlines the key characteristics of the teaching of mathematics as involving problems with more than one possible answer, using different ways to do a problem, communicating in and talking about mathematics, and understanding the importance of sense making in mathematics.

The author underscores the important role that parents can play in supporting their children's learning of mathematics by keeping a positive attitude toward the subject, by engaging in conversations about their mathematics learning, and by making connections to uses of mathematics in everyday life. The book provides some concrete suggestions for activities and games that parents can do with their children based on their age and the grade they are in (all the way through high school). It also provides suggestions on how to help their children with homework without actually doing it for them.

In chapter 2, the author discusses the big ideas in mathematics across the grades and explains the rather technical language used in the Common Core State Standards document. The chapter also describes the shifts in emphasis in the recent years, such as fewer topics per grade level but more in depth, as well as the mathematical practices ("math habits of mind"). The book is filled with suggestions for what parents can do at different stages ("parents can . . ."). A key idea in the book is the importance of parents discussing and talking about mathematics with their children.

Chapters 3, 4, and 5 each begins with an overview of the key content for the different grade bands. Then, the chapters present a variety of classroom-based scenarios with ideas on how parents can support and extend these kinds of activities at home, emphasizing aspects that may be different from their experience and the importance of making sense. Chapter 6 focuses entirely on activities that parents can do with their children, once again emphasizing a key message in this book: the importance of parents and children having conversations about mathematics.

Underscored in this book is the need for school and home to connect when it comes to children's learning of mathematics. The book promotes such a connection with suggestions for parents to engage with their children in mathematical activities that will both support their current learning and expand it. Furthermore, it provides a clear overview of the current ideas in mathematics teaching and learning, thus making it a valuable resource for parents.

Marta Civil
Professor of Mathematics Education and Roy F. Graesser Endowed Chair
Department of Mathematics
The University of Arizona

Preface

"Help me, to help her!" is a plea from thousands of parents who are frustrated trying to help their children with math. A perspective often heard from parents is:

> We don't know how to help our children anymore. The way I was taught to approach certain problems is not how kids are taught to approach them today. The way kids are taught today is more conceptual and inquiry based, whereas we [parents] learned in a more direct way, sort of "here's how you solve this problem, now do it."

As a fellow parent and educator who has listened to parents' voices for close to three decades, whether on the school dismissal corner or at parent-teacher conferences, it is understood that parents care, and they want to support their children in making sense of math.

However, unfamiliarity with math learning environments can be a source of frustration that causes parents to either disengage from children's learning or assist children in ways that contradict classroom practices. Neither option benefits children; hence, this book was written; because *Parents Matter*.

Parents are those social factors in the lives of their children who can positively influence their math achievement. Parents possess "funds of knowledge," meaning accumulated social capital and skills used to navigate everyday life (Jeynes, 2010). These skills, when connected with children's school lives, cultivate success.

One does not need a degree in math to provide support! What one needs is a guidebook filled with good questions to pose, tips for supporting math thinking and general attitudes about math, and an "insider's view" into what math teaching and learning looks like in today's classrooms. This book serves as that guidebook, and its author invites parents to use it while making sense of math with children.

Introduction

This book is a parents' guidebook filled with descriptions about the big math ideas children learn in Grades kindergarten through 8, how they learn about these ideas, and how their parents can support such learning at home. Chapter 1 includes a description about *how* and *why* math teaching has changed through the years. The chapter highlights the positive influence that parents can have on their children's math achievement and shares an overview of supportive home practices.

Chapter 2 outlines the big math ideas taught across the grades. It provides rationale for the current shifts in math learning environments and offers guidelines on how to support these shifts at home. The chapter concludes with a discussion about the math practices, or habits of mind, teachers seek to cultivate among students, along with ways with which parents at home can reinforce teachers' efforts.

Chapters 3 through 5 offer detailed descriptions about how big math ideas develop in Grades kindergarten through 2, 3 through 5, and 6 through 8, respectively. A sampling of grade-level examples, entitled *Classroom Scenes*, provides an insider's view into how math content unfolds in specific grade-level classrooms. Coupled with these scenes are guidelines for parents, entitled *Parents Can*, that direct parents' efforts to support classroom learning at home.

Chapter 6 is termed "Collaborative Anchor Tasks," for the ability of the tasks to connect home and classroom across the grades. The tasks provide entry points for engaging in conversation about math thinking in ways that support the emotional quality of parent-child collaborations. In other words, the tasks encourage participants to celebrate multiple ways of making sense of math, as opposed to debating about whose way is better.

Chapter 1

Teaching and Learning Math

Oftentimes, parents ask *why* math is taught differently from when they themselves were in school. This chapter begins with a description about just that—*how* and *why* math teaching and learning has changed through the years. In keeping with the title of this book, *Parents Matter*, this chapter provides details regarding parents' influence, as social factors, on their child's achievement with math. In the conclusion, an overview of home practices is provided to empower you, as your child's supportive learning partner, in helping make your children make sense of math.

LANDSCAPES THROUGH THE YEARS

Math teaching in the United States has changed dramatically through the years; if you are like the parents mentioned in the opening sentence of the chapter, you would know that today's learning environments are very different from those you experienced as a student. Such unfamiliarity can cause confusion and anxiety about how and why children learn math the way they do today. To provide justification for the evolving nature of math teaching and learning, a historical account of the developing learning landscapes is provided in this section.

Let's begin with the 1940s, a period of time described as one of complacency. Drill and practice methods of teaching permeated classrooms and were accepted without debate. Concerns arose though in the 1950s, labeled as a period of awakening. The Russian satellite Sputnik was launched, and this historical event caused Americans to see themselves as taking a backseat to the accomplishments of others.

Educators began questioning their existing math instructional materials and teaching practices. Consequently, the 1960s, sometimes referred to as a period of overreaction, were filled with changes in teaching styles. Educators became disturbed when they saw that their students viewed math as a subject consisting only of isolated bits of information that needed to be memorized. Hence, drill and practice exercises were replaced with teaching methods that nurtured conceptual understanding. In other words, enabling students to understand math ideas became the focus of instruction, and concrete models served as tools for developing understanding.

Unfortunately, computational accuracy became underemphasized well into the 1970s and this resulted in students' lack of efficiency with computational procedures for addition, subtraction, multiplication, and division. Therefore, rote memorization of math facts once again gained prominence, which meant that the 1980s were a period of turmoil for math education.

Educators debated over methods for learning math. What was better? Focusing on computational fluencies by having children repeatedly use procedures given to them by teachers or focusing on conceptual understanding by guiding children's ability to apply and justify their work when doing math?

The resolution came in 1989 from the National Council of Teachers of Mathematics (NCTM). This organization shed light on the fact that students meaningfully learn math when the focus is on *both* conceptual understanding and computational fluencies. In addition, NCTM stressed that the process of sequencing and application of conceptual understanding and computational fluencies across the grades influences children's ability to make sense of the math they learn in school.

NCTM reframed instructional materials and evaluation standards for prekindergarten (pre-K) to Grade 12. Instruction moved away from a transmission model, a model in which passive learning and a telling approach to teaching existed, to a constructivist model, a model in which learners actively participate with the teacher to solve problems, engage in inquiry, and construct knowledge.

The role of the teacher shifted away from that of filling children's minds with information through telling as if they were pouring soup into a pot. Teachers instead began to focus on enabling children to achieve an in-depth understanding of math ideas and higher-order thinking skills through active engagement in math explorations. All math educators were charged with developing children's conceptual understanding, computational fluencies, and problem-solving abilities in ways that connected math with the real world.

NCTM understood that with the responsibility of delivering such meaningful math experiences came the challenge of planning instructional time in a way that important math topics were taught effectively and in depth.

This leading organization therefore recommended areas of emphasis within each grade from pre-K through Grade 8.

NCTM recommended clear, consistent priorities for a coherent math curriculum across the United States that actually initiated the crafting of the current Common Core State Standards for Mathematics (CCSSM). As outlined by the CCSSM, daily math learning experiences build upon each other in a sequential manner so that children's higher-order thinking skills and applications of mathematics develop across the grades.

Teachers craft lessons so that children develop understanding through stages of learning that move from concretely manipulating objects to modeling math ideas, to representing those ideas through pictures, to ultimately solving math problems symbolically. Teachers do not tell children what to do; rather, teachers predominately guide children's concrete explorations of and conclusions about math ideas.

Children's curiosities are tapped into and their thinking stimulated by engaging them in tasks that involve looking for patterns and discovering relationships. They are encouraged to take risks, and mistakes are viewed as opportunities for learning. In fact, teachers guide students to use incorrect thinking to correct mistakes and deepen understanding.

It is also commonplace for children to solve math problems that have more than one right answer or more than one correct method of solution. Such occurrences bring different perspectives for solving math problems into classroom learning.

Communication is a key element of learning math. Through written and verbal expression, students clarify their thinking in a manner that contributes significantly to conceptual understanding. For example, rather than using instructional time by asking children to silently complete workbook pages filled with repetitive examples, teachers can pose probing questions to facilitate intellectual discussions about different ways to think about key math examples relevant to specific learning objectives.

These current approaches to teaching and learning math support children's ability to collectively use thinking strategies. Such environments motivate children to inquire about math ideas both independently and collaboratively. In addition, this active nature of making sense of math promotes children's (a) retention of material learned, (b) problem-solving abilities, (c) attitudes about themselves as learners of math, and (d) real-life applications of math.

The value of drill and practice is still recognized; in fact, it is essential for attaining computational fluencies. Research in the field of math education informs educators that children's computational fluencies must stem from conceptual understanding. Otherwise, children will not know why the math they commit to memory makes sense.

For example, knowing both *how* to add fractions with common denominators and *why* using common denominators makes sense for that computational procedure demonstrates complete mastery of that topic. If all we expect children to do is implement the computational rules, they won't know why the rules work. In turn, children's ability to apply and justify their work is placed at risk, oftentimes confusing them regarding computational rules because deep understanding of these rules is lacking.

To summarize, instruction has moved beyond mechanical implementation of math procedures. Instruction now focuses on building conceptual understanding along with computational fluencies and real-world applications. Children today construct math ideas and procedures from concrete experiences. Teachers do less telling and more guiding of children's thinking so that math makes sense and has purpose.

PARENTS MATTER

As described in the previous section, teachers today seek to promote math as a tool for thought, rather than as a set of rules and procedures to memorize. Their aim is to develop mathematical thinkers who can solve problems in ways that go beyond just number crunching with memorized procedures; and critical to achieving this goal are the parents!

Both finding success with and enjoying math depend on the learning environment crafted for children in school *and* at home. Parents, meaning adults who play active roles in children's home lives, are those influential social factors who can either support or unravel at home what is learned in the classroom. For example, when parents assist their children by posing thought-provoking questions or breaking down a problem into smaller, more manageable pieces, they help organize mathematical thinking (Walker, Shenker, and Hoover-Dempsey, 2010).

When parents adjust their assistance to match that of their children's current abilities, they scaffold thinking to higher levels. In addition, when parents create home learning environments that nurture self-confidence, they help reduce math anxiety, and in turn, cultivate conditions for academic success, especially with higher levels of math (Vukovic, Roberts, and Wright, 2013). Such forms of support depict the "quality" of assistance parents can give that is just as important, if not more, as the quantity of assistance.

Now, you may say, "Numbers scare me," "I'm not a math person," or "I hate math." If so, please do not advertise this in front of your child because low student academic achievement has been found to correlate with negative family attitudes and beliefs about math. A recent study discussed parents' math anxieties being passed down to children (Vasquez-Salgado and Greenfield, 2015).

If you view yourself as weak in math, please understand that ability in math is not hereditary. Partnering with your child and, in turn, your child's teacher allows an entire learning community to benefit as everyone joins together to make sense out of math. You, as parent, possess "funds of knowledge," meaning accumulated social capital and skills used to navigate everyday life (Jeynes, 2010). You can share such knowledge with your child in ways that connect what you know and how you came to know it with your child's current learning environment.

Just by starting a conversation with your child about his or her math thinking helps to organize ideas, solidify understanding, and even redirect misunderstanding. By looking for similarities and differences in how you and your child approach math problems can deepen both of your understanding about math.

PRODUCTIVELY SUPPORTING YOUR CHILD WITH MATH

Parents often request (a) content information, (b) online resources, (c) strategies for helping with homework, and (d) ways to communicate with children about math. This section responds to these requests; the productive action steps outlined in this section are those recommended by the NCTM (NCTM, 2004). In later chapters, more specific guidelines will be explained while digging deeper into grade-level content.

Stay Positive!

As previously noted, your attitude can very easily become your child's attitude. So, be positive about your child's math ability and praise his or her efforts and accomplishments. Children need to understand that math can be challenging at times; struggles with math should not be viewed as lack of ability. Tell your child that productive struggle with math is part of the thinking process that helps him or her make sense of the math they are learning.

Encourage your child to persevere with the math that he or she finds hard, just as one perseveres with a challenging sport. Share with your child that persistence and hard work are essential for success. Particularly in the middle- and high-school years, a child will appreciate and find pleasure in doing math if he or she is challenged and supported to persevere both in school and at home.

If your child's interest in math starts to fade, shed light on the fact that middle-school math lays the foundation that determines success in all high-school math courses. It can be challenging to maintain your child's interest in math as he or she gets older. Friends and outside activities can divert attention. In turn, your degree of involvement may vary as your child moves to higher grades.

For example, it may be harder to get to know your child's multiple teachers in middle and high school. Your confidence with the type of math your child is learning may decrease. Also, now your child may not want you as involved in his or her schoolwork as you were in the past.

Although such changes may occur, your support as *parent still matters* as it did in the elementary school years. Guidelines to continue supporting your child as he or she gets older are as follows:

- Support your child in developing good study habits and time management skills. For example, teach him or her to not wait till the last minute to study for a math test or complete a math project. Giving him or her latitude in making decisions about schoolwork completion is good; however, have high expectations for the work he or she produces and hold them accountable for completing quality work in time.
- Keep lines of communication open by having conversations with your child about the importance of learning math. Discuss any related issues he or she may be encountering.
- Encourage your child to seek help from his or her math teacher and peers. Reinforce that learning math goes beyond just natural ability; it involves confidence, persistence, and hard work.

Connect Math with Daily Life!

Young children are naturally curious and want to explore their surroundings. They actually come to school with a substantial amount of math knowledge and understanding from their concrete play explorations prior to beginning formal schooling. As children move through the elementary years, they may begin to lose enthusiasm for math, especially during the middle grades, if they do not see connections with the real world.

So, please help your child see math in his or her everyday life so that their zeal for the subject remains alive! Some examples include:

- Determining total costs for store purchases
- Determining distances while reading a map
- Creating a budget
- Determining sale prices
- Creating schedules

Below are some ways, arranged according to grade-level bands, by which you and your child can connect math with everyday life.

Elementary School Years

- Have fun counting out loud together anything that your child encounters—number of blocks he or she owns, number of steps he or she climbs, or number of crackers he or she eats.
- Sort and classify objects into sets, such as cars, blocks, dolls, or stuffed animals. Have conversations about size or quantity by posing questions such as, Which is larger? Which is largest? Which is smaller? Which is smallest? Do you have more cars or more stuffed animals? Are there fewer dolls or fewer blocks?
- Go hunting for shapes and numbers. Look for two- and three-dimensional shapes such as squares and cubes. Look for numbers in your neighborhood such as addresses, license plates, phone numbers, and weather forecasts; talk about what those numbers mean and how they are used in everyday life.
- While setting the dinner table, ask your child to fold the napkins as rectangles one day and triangles another day. Ask him or her to find the number of chairs to match the number of plates at the table. Also engage him or her in determining the number of knives, forks, and spoons needed.
- Sorting laundry before washing can turn into a fun math game with your child sorting the clothes by colors or by family members. He or she can also sort groceries while helping you put them away.
- Involve your child in counting money by asking him or her to help count the money you have in your wallet. While shopping, ask him or her to tell you the prices of items you need to purchase. You can even set up a play store or organize a garage sale where he or she can get involved in using money while making purchases and selling products.
- Have your child help you with measures during everyday activities such as cooking, gardening, making crafts, and doing home improvements. When you measure, use measuring tools such rulers, yardsticks, meter sticks, tape measures, measuring cups, and scales. And measure in both customary (inches, cups, pounds, etc.) and metric (centimeters, liters, grams, etc.) units.
- Have your child keep charts or graphs to organize information. For example, keeping track of how many different types of coins, stamps, or bottle caps he or she is collecting helps to organize and explain data.
- Practice estimation by guessing the number of pieces of candy in a jar. Discuss strategies you can use to come up with reasonable estimates.

Middle- and High-School Years

- Point out the math involved in schedules such as television guides and transportation timetables for trains and buses.

- Discuss what the data shown on charts, tables, and graphs in newspapers and magazines mean. For example, for a graph that shows people's use of technology (cell phones, laptops, social media, etc.), you might ask your child such questions as, "How many hours a day do people use their cell phone, and why is this information useful?" and "What type of social media is most often used and why is this information useful?"
- Have your child budget his or her allowance for making personal purchases. Guide him or her to compare prices and determine possible savings for items that go on sale. For example, encourage him or her to determine savings on sneakers that have 30 percent off.
- Open a bank account and have your child keep track of deposits, withdrawals, and interest. Investigate other investment options such as certificates of deposit and money market funds. Explore stock and bond options, even if only in an imaginary way.
- Sports enthusiasts can keep track of scores and statistics by collecting data from newspapers and the Web. Use the collected data to make predictions. Create graphs that show a team or team player's performance over time.
- Use household situations as teachable moments. For example, wise spending, refinancing your home, leasing or financing a car, acquiring a credit card, and getting a home equity loan are opportunities for conversation with your child about financial processes and outcomes. A very useful resource for supporting your child's understanding of money and finance is the website www.themint.org.
- Investigate the college-related expenses by developing a chart to compare cost of tuition and room and board at different colleges, along with scholarships and other forms of financial aid.

Make Math Enjoyable!

You want your child to associate math with pleasant experiences. So play board games and solve puzzles, all the time pointing out the math involved so as to enhance your child's thinking and pleasure with math. Following are tasks that families have found very enjoyable due to the tasks' ability to spark math conversations among family members.

Today's Date

This game involves representing the numeral of a date in multiple ways. It will help build your child's sense of number and provide opportunities to communicate about multiple correct solutions. It is applicable to any day of the year and is appropriate for all grade levels. You simply offer the following statement: Today is _____.

For example, if the date is September 28, the task is to represent 28 in multiple ways.

Following are some responses.

20 + 8	32 − 4
XXVIII	I have $35 and spend $7. How much do I have left?
81 ÷ 9 + 19	28/1
(5 × 5) + 3	2 tens 8 ones
3x + 9 = 93	

Which One Doesn't Belong?

This game involves comparing and contrasting four examples to determine one example that differs from the others. As with *Today's Date*, this game provides opportunities to communicate about multiple correct solutions. It can also spark conversation about multiple reasons for a single solution. A sample game and related responses follow.

Responses:

- 18 + 14, because it is the only example where both numbers contain double digits
- 6 + 4, because it is the only example that is written horizontally
- 16 − 9, because it is the only example without a 4 in it
- 16 − 9, because it is the only example that has a prime (number divisible by only 1 and itself) answer
- 8 + 4, because it is the only example that contains one numeral that is half the other.

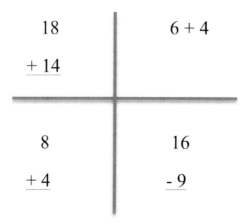

Figure 1.1 **(Which One Doesn't Belong?).** *Source:* Regina M. Mistretta

Parents find this game enhancing the emotional quality of conversations with their children because of its multiple approaches and multiple solutions. In other words, the task reduces anxieties that can arise when determining only one correct answer, or only one correct way of arriving at an answer.

It helps shift the parent-child conversation away from a "my way or the highway" dialogue to one that celebrates diverse ways of thinking. Parents and children can share and appreciate each other's contributions to the conversation, rather than pit one solution or method of solution against another.

Examples for your use at different grade-level bands can be found at http://tinyurl.com/ltpw6af. Although these examples are categorized, each of them can be used to compare or contrast the appearance of examples for the purpose of supporting math reasoning at all grade levels.

Discuss Math-Related Careers!

Point out to your child the different jobs that involve math; a wide variety of careers stem from math. Discuss the math that you and other family members use at work and at home, as well as how the people your child knows use math (the bus driver, store keeper, baby sitter, mail carrier, etc.)

Your child's interests and aspirations may change during and after high school; hence, research with your child various career and education options. Discuss with your school administrator and teacher what your child should be doing now to prepare for the careers he or she is interested in pursuing in the future. A good resource for learning about math-related careers is *Career Ideas for Kids Who Like Math*, a book by Diane Lindsey Reeves.

Hold High Expectations!

Traditionally in North America, a view that only some students are capable of succeeding in math has permeated society. This is simply not true! Math is accessible to all. You wouldn't accept your child saying, "They just can't read." So don't accept him or her saying, "They just can't do math."

Your attitude about your child's ability to succeed in math is essential to his or her achievement. Communicate high expectations to your child. Advocate for your child among teachers, counselors, and administrators so he or she receives equal opportunities in math. Express your desire for him or her to take appropriately challenging math classes each year, all the way through high school.

Guide Homework, Don't Do It!

Homework can be the cause of friction in households. Remain calm and remember whose homework it is. Being a "helicopter parent" and taking over homework completion for your child isn't productive. Doing homework for your child, or telling your child how to do it, only encourages him or her to give up or to rely on you for answers. In turn, the tendency to persevere with challenging problems will diminish, or not start at all.

Children need to be resourceful, persistent, and confident. To cultivate such dispositions, you as parent need to "guide on the side." Ultimately, your role is to support and encourage your child to be accountable for his or her learning. Getting frustrated with your child or yourself for not knowing the math isn't productive support. Following are descriptions of how your support should look.

You can facilitate your child's homework by asking good questions and listening. Simply asking your child to explain aloud his or her thinking can be powerful. As previously explained and worth repeating, opportunities for children to speak and write about their thinking provides opportunities to organize thoughts, clarify thinking, and even self-correct misunderstanding.

Oftentimes, parents worry about not having answers to children's questions. You need not worry; your role is not to have all the answers all the time. Rather, your role is to support your child in determining what he or she doesn't know. Sometimes children are so confused that they can't even craft a specific question to pose to their parent or teacher.

So, discussing math thinking at home grants your child the time to determine where he or she is struggling and to craft question(s) he or she can pose in school. You learn together when your child comes home from school and shares the responses to the questions you helped him or her craft.

Asking Good Questions!

Communication is essential for knowing the math your child learns in school, as well as how he or she is making sense of that math. Below are questions for you to pose, as recommended by the NCTM (NCTM, 2004).

Questions to Pose to Your Child

- What new math idea did you learn today?
- What did you find most interesting about what you learned in math class today?
- What was most challenging about what you learned in math class today?
- What did you feel you did best at in math class today?
- What was most enjoyable about learning math today?

Questions to Pose When Supporting Math Homework

- What are you working on?
- What are the directions saying?

- What words or directions are confusing you?
- How should you begin?
- What do you already know that can help you?
- What have you already done?
- Can we look for help in your textbook or class notes?
- Have you done a similar problem?
- Can you draw a picture or make a diagram to show what you are thinking about?
- Can you explain what the teacher said in class today?
- Where are you getting stuck?
- Where can we look for help online?
- What questions could you ask your teacher?

Questions to Pose About Your Child's Math Program

- Do all students receive the same math instruction? If not, how are learning environments designed?
- How does the math program challenge my child?
- How does the math program address my child's needs?
- How are families involved in the math program?
- What technology is used?
- When and how will I know about my child's progress?
- Where can we find more problems or resources to use for practice?
- Is a homework support structure maintained for students' use?
- What are some math online resources we can use?
- Are there any remediation or enrichment programs offered at school?
- Do the children participate in any math competitions or contests?
- Do any nearby colleges or universities offer remediation or enrichment programs?

Questions to Pose to Your Child's Math Teacher

- What math will my child learn this year?
- What instructional materials will my child use to learn math this year?
- What will math homework look like this year, and how much time should my child spend on math homework?
- How are math grades determined, and what graded work is sent home?
- How often, when, and how will I be informed about my child's math progress?
- How do I schedule time for conversation with you about my child's math learning?
- What, if any, standardized math tests will my child take this year?
- What can I do to help my child in math?
- How can I support you, the teacher?

REFERENCES

Vasquez-Salgado, Y. and P. M. Greenfield. "Exploring Home-School Value Conflicts: Implications for Academic Achievement and Well-Being Among Latino First-Generation College Students." *Journal of Adolescent Research*, 30.3 (2015): 271–305.

Jeynes, W. H. "The Salience of the Subtle Aspects of Parental Involvement and Encouraging that Involvement: Implications for School-Based Programs." *Teachers College Record*, 112 (2010): 747–74.

NCTM (2004). *A Family's Guide: Fostering your Child's Success in School Mathematics*. Reston, VA: Author.

Vukovic, R. K., S. O. Roberts, and L. G. Wright. "From Parental Involvement to Children's Mathematical Performance: The Role of Mathematics Anxiety." *Early Education and Development*, 24 (2013): 446–67.

Walker, J., S. Shenker, and K. Hoover-Dempsey. "Why Do Parents Become Involved in their Children's Education? Implications for School Counselors." *Professional School Counseling*, 14 (2010): 27–41.

Chapter 2

Supporting Your Child's
Math Learning Terrain

As underscored in chapter 1, children are best positioned to make sense of math when both the classroom and home learning environments connect. This chapter continues to support you as parent in helping your child make sense of math.

The big math ideas being taught across the grades are explained in this chapter to provide an overview of what math content is taught at what grade levels. The rationale behind the shifts in how children learn math today are discussed, along with guidelines on how you can support these shifts at home. Finally, the math practices, or "habits of mind," teachers seek to cultivate in classrooms are explained along with ways that you can reflect these classroom efforts at home.

BIG IDEAS ACROSS THE GRADES

The term *content domains*, in the CCSSM, refers to the big math ideas your child is learning about in school. Existing within each content domain are specific learning objectives called *standards*. When certain standards relate to each other, they are considered a *cluster*. A cluster of standards under the domain of measurement and data are as follows:

• Measurement and data
  ◦ Measure lengths indirectly and by iterating length units.
  ◦ Tell and write time.
  ◦ Represent and interpret data.

You may be saying to yourself, *What does "measure lengths indirectly and by iterating length units" mean?* Indirect measurement tasks generally involve comparing the lengths of two objects that are not lined up beside each other by using a third object other than a ruler. Iterating is the mental activity of building up the length of an object with equal-sized units of another object, for example, lining up equal-sized paper clips lengthwise to determine the number of paper clips needed to measure the length of one pencil.

When terminology such as that described above is unfamiliar to you, inquire about their meanings from your child's teacher. Khan Academy (www.khanacademy.org) is also a wonderful resource that clearly defines math terms. Chapters 3 through 5 of this book unfold math content according to grade-level bands, specifically, Grades kindergarten through 2, Grades 3 through 5, and Grades 6 through 8. What math content looks like when taught in classrooms, along with defined terminology, and how *Parents Can* support these classroom scenes are provided in these chapters.

SHIFTS IN MATH LEARNING ENVIRONMENTS

Fueled by research about how best to learn math, the NCTM has advocated for decades that math classrooms should no longer be viewed as collections of individuals, but rather as communities of learners. Instead of teachers being the sole authority for right answers, students should use their own logic and mathematical evidence to verify answers.

NCTM has consistently recommended that mathematical reasoning replace mere memorization of procedures so that mechanical finding of answers can shift to conjecturing, inventing, and problem-solving as means for arriving at answers. In addition, rather than treating math as a body of isolated concepts and procedures, math ideas should be connected and applied.

The current shifts in math classroom environments reflect NCTM's recommendations, namely, focus, coherence, fluency, deep understanding, application, and dual intensity. In this section, what these shifts look like in the classroom is explained and guidelines for supporting such classroom learning at home provided.

Focus

A common criticism of past math curriculum in the United States is that it was "a mile wide and an inch deep." Because each academic year contained several topics, there just wasn't time for teachers to address those topics in depth. This was also the reason that students tended not to master all the topics, resulting in teachers repeating previously taught topics the following year. Consequently, educators in other countries viewed math education in the United States as *covering* math topics, as opposed to *teaching* topics in meaningful ways.

In today's math classrooms, instruction is better focused so that students learn more about less. In other words, they spend more time on fewer concepts because teachers are now focusing instructional time on priority concepts. Such a shift enables the students to (a) attain deep foundational understanding and skills and (b) transfer these understanding and skills across math topics and grades. For example, learning about multiplication and division of fractions in Grade 5 supports their understanding of ratios and proportional reasoning in Grade 6.

Parents Can:
- Inquire from your child's teacher about the priority work for his or her grade level.
- Spend time with your child on that priority work. When your child completes homework, support him or her by using the questions included in chapter 1. You can also access content-specific support materials from www.nctm.org, www.engageny.org, and www.annenberglearner.org. Once on the website, type the topic and grade level you need resources for into the search box.
- Discuss your child's progress with priority work with his or her teacher and ask how you can continue supporting your child.

Coherence

To minimize repetition of topics, coherency in skills exists across grade levels. In other words, math topics are aligned across the grades so that the knowledge of your child builds up from year to year in a sequenced learning progression. Teachers connect content from a prior year with the current grade level so that understanding and skills develop to higher and higher levels of math thinking.

It can be thought of as opening a window. A kindergarten teacher's instruction opens the window so far. The first grade teacher is charged with knowing what was learned in kindergarten, and how it was learned, so he or she can build upon that learning environment and, in turn, further open up that window. Each standard is not a new event, but an extension of previous learning.

Parents Can:
- Speak with your child's teachers about what your child struggled with the previous year, and how it will affect his or her learning this year. Such conversation can help you determine possible gaps that you can help fill to support your child's conceptual understanding and related skills.

Fluency

To cultivate speed and accuracy in solving math problems, time is spent practicing skills with intensity (in high volume). Teachers will structure class time and homework time for students to memorize, through repetition, basic facts so that they are more able to understand and manipulate more complex math topics. For example, mastery of multiplication facts positions a child to perform long division successfully.

Parents Can:
• Become knowledgeable of all the fluencies for your child's grade level through conversation with his or her teacher.
• Ask your child's teacher to help you prioritize those fluencies in need of mastery.
• Discuss with your child the meaning of basic facts. For example, $4 \times 3 = 12$ means 4 groups of 3 making 12 in all. Use pictures to represent the facts, and ultimately discuss and practice the facts with your child to support both their conceptual understanding and computational fluency.

Deep Understanding

Children must deeply know math in order to do math in a meaningful manner. Hence, classroom instruction isn't merely to provide computational procedures for children to use when solving math problems. Rather, instruction serves to justify why those procedures make sense. Teachers expect their students to demonstrate deep levels of conceptual understanding of priority concepts. Therefore, your child will be called upon to articulate his or her understanding through modeling, verbal explanation, and written expression.

In addition, because children learn in different ways and at different paces, teachers create opportunities to understand math concepts and procedures from a variety of entry points. Adapting instruction to meet diverse learning styles helps ensure that each child understands the material before moving on to further topics.

Now your child may come home saying, "My teacher won't tell me how to solve this problem." Please don't become agitated by that teacher's reluctance to give answers and methods of solution; he or she is allowing your child to grapple with ideas, investigate methods of solution, determine what works and why, as well as what doesn't work and why, for particular math situations.

Your child is in good hands. Rather than spoon-feeding information that will most likely be forgotten, today's math teachers guide students to actively construct and ultimately retain knowledge. Yes, it is a rigorous learning environment. Ponder this anonymous Chinese proverb:

Tell me, I'll forget.
Show me, I'll remember.
Involve me, I'll understand.

Teachers teach more than "how to get the answer." Teachers support their students in accessing concepts from a number of perspectives so that math is deeply understood and perceived as a way of thinking, rather than as isolated bits of information and procedures to memorize.

Parents Can:
• Determine whether or not your child really knows the answer by engaging him or her in conversation about their math thinking and written work. Providing as many opportunities as possible for your child to discuss their grade-level math with you can make a world of difference.

You need not have mastery of the content yourself. Just carving out time for your child to talk with you and write about the math they are learning affords opportunities to clarify their thoughts and correct misunderstandings. For those times when both you and your child are stuck on a math problem, spend time forming the question(s) that can be posed to the teacher.

It can't be stressed enough how valuable it is for your child's conceptual development to have time to communicate with you about the math they are learning in school.

The time you spend with your child discussing his or her thinking can help sort out what your child knows and doesn't know, which, in turn, allows teachers and you to provide the support your child needs.

Application

Children desire purpose for what they learn in school; a common question, particularly from middle-school students, is, "Why do I need to learn this?" Children shouldn't need to settle for a response such as, "It's exercise for your brain."

Through thoughtful planning and selection of meaningful tasks, teachers support students to both independently and collaboratively determine methods of solution for solving relevant everyday math problems. For example, students engage in tasks such as determining a shape for a room that provides the most living space, arranging tables to maximize seating, and investigating factors involved in choosing an appropriate cell phone plan.

Parents Can:
- Regularly point out examples of math used in the world.
- Ask your child about the math that came up during his or her day; share your encounters with math as well.
- Help cultivate an appreciation of math by discussing how it can help answer real-world questions. The website entitled Real-World Math (http://www.nctm.org/Publications/Microsites/Real-World-Math/Worlds-Volume-1/The-Biological-World/) is a wonderful resource for supporting your child's awareness of the purpose for math in supporting solutions to existing societal issues.

Dual Intensity

Dual intensity involves children rigorously practicing the basic arithmetic facts and procedures they have come to deeply understand. Teachers create opportunities for students to participate in "drills," as well as apply understanding and skills while solving problems.

Parents Can:
- Take note of your child's areas of strength and weakness, or his or her "glows" and "grows." Address areas in need of growth with his or her teacher.
- Engage your child in conversation about how the math he or she is learning in school is used in real life.
- Encourage your child to both speak *and* write about his or her math thinking.

MATH HABITS OF MIND

In addition to the content domains and clusters of standards, the CCSSM include math practices involving eight expected behaviors, or habits of mind, for doing math. These practices are also referred to as "processes and proficiencies" (CCSSM, 2010, p. 6).

What these eight habits of mind look like in the classroom is explained in this section, along with how parents can support children in developing these habits at home. Depending on the math problem your child is working on, certain habits of mind will be more relevant to support than others.

You need not try to support all eight habits every time you help your child with a math problem. You can't do everything all the time. What is important is that you familiarize yourself with these thinking habits and support your child in acquiring them as appropriate.

Make Sense of Problems and Persevere in Solving Them

This math practice involves your child being able to explain the meaning of a problem and, in turn, look for ways to start solving it. Rather than simply jumping into a method of solution, your child's teacher will guide him or her to analyze given information, constraints, relationships, and goals.

Your child is expected to first make conjectures about the form and meaning of the solution and then to plan an approach for solving the problem at hand. The teacher guides him or her to consider similar problems and simpler forms of the problem to gain insight into its solution.

Your child monitors and evaluates his or her progress and changes course if necessary. In addition, he or she uses concrete objects or illustrations to think about and solve math problems, as well as checks answers using different methods than those originally used.

The teacher guides rather than tells your child what to do. This positions your child to think harder while strategizing approaches for making sense of the math. He or she needs to be encouraged to persevere as he or she grapples through the learning process.

Parents Can:
• Provide time for your child to discuss with you his or her approaches and solutions.
• Offer guiding feedback. Hold back from giving answers. Be the "guide on the side," rather than "the sage on the stage."
• Solving math problems is a process. Let your child know that thinking about a math problem takes time, and encourage him or her to persevere.

For example, suppose we have the following situation entitled the Animal Pen Problem:

• You have 20 feet of fencing to create square and rectangular pens (enclosed spaces) for animals on a farm. How many ways can you form a pen for the animals? What are the areas of each of the pens you can form?

To support your child in making sense of this problem, you can suggest that he or she draw a picture of one possible way to form an enclosed space that uses all 20 feet of fencing. Such a supportive action step can help him or her to understand the problem and initiate his or her determination of other illustrations that fit the problem.

Figure 2.1 portrays the goal of this task; to develop understanding about how shapes with the same *perimeter* (distance around) can have varying *areas* (amount of space covered in square units).

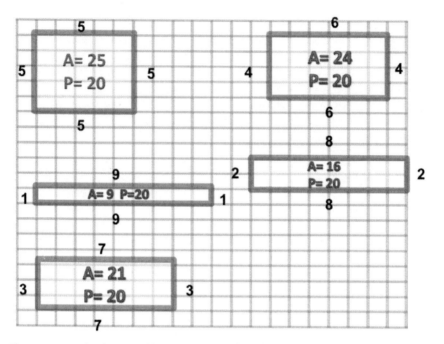

Figure 2.1   (Animal Pen Problem). *Source*: Regina M. Mistretta

Reason Abstractly and Quantitatively

Your child is guided in school to make sense of quantities and their relationships. He or she conceptualizes a given situation by representing it with symbols. He or she reasons numerically by considering the units involved and attends to the meanings of quantities, not just how to compute them. He or she is also guided to use flexibly different rules for addition, subtraction, multiplication, and division; for example, the order of the numbers they add or multiply doesn't change the answer (7 + 5 = 5 + 7 and 7 × 5 = 5 × 7).

Parents Can:
• Provide manipulative materials (moveable concrete objects), drawings, or online images or tools for your child to model a math problem he or she is working on.
• Have your child explain a model or representation he or she created for a math problem. During the explanation, guide his or her thinking by posing related questions. Remember, refrain from telling how to do it!

For example, in the Animal Pen Problem above, you can support your child to think abstractly by helping him or her create all five representations.

You are helping him or her to visualize the different enclosed spaces, along with the related perimeters and areas.

When you guide your child to form sentences for computing the perimeters of the representations using addition or both addition and multiplication, you are supporting his or her quantitative reasoning. You can further develop their quantitative reasoning by discussing the multiplication computation sentence for finding the areas for the enclosed spaces (length times width).

Construct Viable Arguments and Critique the Reasoning of Others

Your child uses his or her prior knowledge to make a case, or to justify solutions to math problems solved in school. He or she makes conjectures and develops a logical sequence of steps to explore the truth of his or her assumptions. Your child will present his or her case to teachers and peers, as well as respond to peers' justifications. In addition, he or she is placed in situations where he or she compares the strengths and weaknesses of two possible justifications.

Parents Can:
- Prompt discussions with your child by posing questions about his or her approaches and solution(s) to problems.
- Encourage your child to provide justifications for why certain strategies work, as well as why certain strategies work better than others.
- Share your own approaches, solutions, and justifications for math problems. Engage in conversation with your child about how your reasoning compares or contrasts with his or hers.

For example, in the Animal Pen Problem above, you can prompt discussion with your child about why the different numerical computations for the perimeter and area of each animal pen work. Have your child use the representations he or she drew to justify the computational procedure used. In addition, talk about why one can calculate the perimeters of the enclosed spaces by just adding or by both adding and multiplying.

Model with Math

The math problems your child solves in school apply to everyday life. When engaged in problem-solving, your child is guided to make assumptions and approximations to simplify a problem. He or she identifies important quantities and uses tools to map out relationships among those quantities. In addition, your child reflects on the reasonableness of his or her answers.

Parents Can:

- Provide contexts for your child to apply the math he or she learns in school. In other words, connect the math your child is using to everyday situations at home so he or she sees a purpose for the math he or she is learning in school.
- Help your child target necessary information for solving a problem.
- Encourage your child to use simpler numbers to help him or her understand a problem and determine a method for solving it.

For example, in the Animal Pen Problem above, math is applied to a real-life situation. You can build upon this application by discussing other contexts in everyday life that involve calculating perimeter and area, such as a fence for your home, a carpet for a room, or a garden space for your backyard or neighborhood green space.

In addition, by reinforcing with your child the reasonableness of the dimensions for each of the solutions to the Animal Pen Problem, as well as other related real-life situations, you are supporting your child's ability to accurately model math ideas.

Use Appropriate Tools Strategically

Your child has access to a variety of instructional tools in school such as manipulatives, drawings, and technology. He or she considers these tools and chooses the most appropriate one for solving certain math problems. He or she estimates to detect possible errors and uses instructional tools to help visualize, explore, and compare information.

Parents Can:

- Provide instructional tools to your child to use at home when solving math problems, such as a ruler, protractor, calculator, measuring tape, counting blocks, and math-related software or websites. Ask his or her teacher which tools are relevant to your child's grade level.
- Engage in using these tools with your child to support him or her in making sense of the math problems they seek to solve.

For example, in the Animal Pen Problem above, using graph paper to illustrate the solutions supports your child in counting and justifying a perimeter of 20. In addition, the graph paper, with its square units, supports your child's understanding of (a) area as the amount of square units taken up by each enclosed space and (b) the involved computation, as he or she first counts the squares within each enclosed space and then determines related computational procedures.

Attend to Precision

Your child is expected to precisely communicate his or her math thinking to others. He or she uses clear definitions during verbal discussions and in written explanations. Examples include stating the meanings of symbols, specifying units of measure, and labeling axes on graphs. In addition, your child is expected to calculate accurately and efficiently and express numerical answers as precisely as possible.

Parents Can:
- Emphasize the importance of precise communication, including appropriate use of math vocabulary.
- Emphasize the importance of accuracy and efficiency in solutions to problems, including use of estimation and mental math, when appropriate.

For example, in the Animal Pen Problem above, you can support your child's proper use of math vocabulary by guiding him or her to accurately use the terms *perimeter* and *area* when explaining solutions. You can support your child in precisely communicating his or her mathematical thinking by asking him or her to provide reasons for the different computational methods that can be used to calculate the perimeter and area for each of the enclosed spaces.

Look For and Make Use of Structure

Your child is encouraged in school to look for and explain patterns and structure within the math he or she is learning. He or she is guided to shift perspective and look at things as single objects, or as composed of several objects. In addition, he or she is guided to explain why and when properties of addition, subtraction, multiplication, and division exist in math problems.

Parents Can:
- Engage in conversation with your child about patterns or relationships he or she notices among number facts.
- Discuss with your child ways to sort shapes according to different characteristics (lengths of sides, number of angles, sizes, etc.).
- Help your child think about the meanings of individual components of math problems and about how those components work together.

For example, in the Animal Pen Problem above, you can support your child's determination of patterns by asking him or her to explain what they notice about the perimeter and area of the possible solutions. Such direction positions your child to determine that the area of the enclosed spaces can vary even though the perimeter remains the same.

A follow-up to the original task can involve designing rectangular pens where the area remains constant at 20, and you and your child explore what happens to the corresponding perimeters. In this case, you can support your child in discovering that the largest perimeter exists for the rectangle with the largest length.

In addition, your child's realization of the square shape having the largest area supports real-life applications of area and perimeter. For example, a boy stated during a family mathematics night, "If I get my own room someday, I'm going to ask for the most square-ish one I can get. That nine-by-one design is out of the question. As soon as I get up out of bed, I'll walk into the wall."

Look For and Express Regularity in Repeated Reasoning

Your child reasons in school about varied strategies and methods for solving math problems. He or she notes if calculations are repeated and looks for general methods of solution, as well as shortcuts. In addition, he or she self-assesses to see whether a strategy makes sense while working through it and checks for reasonableness before giving a final answer.

For example, suppose your child notices when dividing 25 by 11 that he or she is repeating the same calculation over and over again. Such observance of the repetition allows him or her to conclude that a repeating decimal exists as an answer. Another example is if your child notices while calculating *slope* (steepness) of a line that his or her answers are the same for any two points on that line.

Parents Can:
- Encourage your child to look for and discuss with you the regularity in his or her reasoning.
- Question your child about why the repetitions he or she notes occur.

For example, in the Animal Pen Problem, you can guide your child's determination of general formulas for finding perimeter and area for rectangles and *squares* (special types of rectangles due to four existing equal sides). For example, asking your child to look for shortcuts for computing the perimeter of the 6 by 4 rectangle directs his or her attention to adding together the doubled lengths and doubled widths.

Chapter 3

Big Math Ideas in Grades K–2

This chapter provides descriptions about how big math ideas develop in Grades kindergarten through 2 (K–2). A sampling of grade-level examples, entitled *Classroom Scenes*, provides an insider's view into how content unfolds in these grade-level classrooms. Coupled with these scenes are guidelines for parents about how to support such learning at home.

DEVELOPING CONTENT

Counting and Cardinality

Counting means saying number names, in standard order, coupling each object counted with one and only one number name, and each number name with one and only one object. *Cardinality* is all about the number of objects in a set. When children *count*, they emphasize or repeat the last word said to mean the total number of objects in a set (*cardinal* number).

In prekindergarten, children learn to use number names and count while singing songs and playing games. In *kindergarten*, number names and the counting sequence are emphasized. Children count by rote from 1 to 100 by tens and also count forward from a given number.

Kindergarteners write *numerals* (symbols), such as 3, to represent the *numbers* (quantities) 0 to 20. Written numerals are matched with quantities of objects the numerals represent. Children analyze relationships between groups of objects and come to understand that each successive numeral refers to a quantity that is one more.

Kindergarten children also start to develop a sense of *conservation*. Conservation means the understanding that the number or amount of something remains the same when spatially rearranged. For example, the number represented by a line of six checkers remains the same when those checkers are spread out. Also the amount of water in a glass remains the same even when that water is poured into a wide pan.

Operations and Algebraic Thinking

Operations refer to the use of numbers to add, subtract, multiply, and divide. *Algebraic thinking* involves children using analytical thinking to learn about algebraic ideas such as expressions representing unknown quantities, expressions involving operations on unknown quantities, and relationships among quantities and expressions.

In *kindergarten*, children use fingers, drawings, rhythms, role-playing, and equations when learning how to join (add) and separate (subtract) objects. They decompose (break apart) numbers less than or equal to 10 by forming pairs in multiple ways. Such activity teaches them to recognize that a set of objects can be broken into smaller groupings and still retain the same quantity of objects. This understanding stems from the idea of conservation described earlier.

Kindergarteners solve word problems involving addition and subtraction with numbers up to 10 using different thinking strategies. They are also given opportunities to model situations involving joining and separating to begin developing fluency with adding and subtracting numbers up to 5.

In *first grade*, work involving addition and subtraction continues. Children solve one- and two-step word problems with numbers up to 100. They develop fluency with addition and subtraction facts with numbers up to 20, again by using thinking strategies.

Second graders come to deeply understand all sums of two one-digit numbers as a result of their experiences during Grades K–2 that involve manipulatives and visual representations. *Digits* mean the numbers 0, 1, 2, 3, 4, 5, 6, 7, 8, and 9. *Second graders* also learn about the concepts of odd and even by pairing objects, counting by 2s, and writing equations. Toward the end of *second grade*, children use arrays to show repeated addition as a foundation for future learning about multiplication.

Number and Operations in Base Ten

The base ten number system, or "place value" system, determines the value of numerals based on their position. For example, 6 has a value of 6 ones or six, whereas 6 in 60 has a value of 6 tens or sixty. A deep understanding of the base ten number system supports computational fluency. Children learn more and more about the base ten number system by seeing its underlying repetitive process of bundling by ten.

Kindergarteners explore numbers from 11 to 19 by composing and decomposing numbers into 10 ones and some additional ones, using manipulatives to model their thinking. Children record their thinking with a drawing or equation such as $17 = 10 + 7$. While exploring real-world problems using a variety of manipulatives, kindergarteners express their reasoning in words. As their vocabulary develops, children become more precise in their explanations and computations.

First graders deepen their understanding of the base ten number system. Through guided learning, they come to recognize the underlying process of repeatedly bundling by ten. As children work through related activities, teachers coach them to share thinking. As a result, *first graders* become proficient in using numbers by reasoning and communicating about the structure and patterns they discover in the number system.

Second graders extend such learning to hundreds. They come to understand that the three digits of a three-digit number represent amounts of hundreds, tens, and ones. They recognize that 100 is the same amount as 10 groups of 10, as well as 100 ones. Children explore and communicate about number patterns while counting with numbers up to 1000. They "count on" from any number and skip count by 5s, 10s, and 100s.

Second graders read and write numbers up to 1000. They compare two three-digit numbers, as well as add and subtract with numbers up to 100. They work with concrete models and drawings to strategize while adding and subtracting numbers up to 1000. In addition, children are called upon to explain why addition and subtraction strategies work.

Measurement and Data

By measuring objects around them, children explore their world. *Measurement* is finding the lengths, height, and weight of objects using units such as centimeters, meters, and grams. Measurement also involves finding elapsed time, or finding time between events using units of seconds, minutes, and hours.

In *kindergarten*, children describe measurable attributes (characteristics) such as length, weight, and color. They may describe one pencil as long and another as short, and one box as heavy and another as light. They may even describe a single object with more than one measurable attribute, such as a small, yellow ball.

Kindergarteners directly compare two objects with a measurable common attribute to determine which has "more" or "less" of an attribute and then describe the difference noted. For example, children may compare heights of family members and describe one family member as "shorter," or line up blocks and determine one row as "a lot shorter" than another. Children compare and contrast objects based on color, size, and shape. They also sort collections of objects according to attributes and organize collections by the amounts they count.

First graders build upon such learning and gain experience using *nonstandard* (e.g., paper clips, cubes, crayons, hands) and *standard* (e.g., centimeters, meters, inches, feet) *units* of measure. They develop measuring skills as they discover how particular units and measuring tools work better than others in different situations.

As children come to know the meaning and processes of measurement, they develop an ability to organize, represent, and interpret real-life *data*, or information, using tally marks, graphs, and charts. *Second graders* use customary (inches, feet, gallons, etc.) and metric (centimeters, meters, liters, etc.) units to measure. They choose an attribute to measure, select an appropriate unit of measure, and determine the number of units.

Second graders measure objects using two units of different lengths, such as meters and centimeters. Doing so teaches them to develop understanding about the importance of the unit used with respect to the attribute being measured.

Second graders predict, estimate units, make connections between number lines and rulers, and use length to solve word problems involving addition and subtraction with numbers up to 100. Children expand their skills at skip counting by 5s to tell and write time from analog and digital clocks to the nearest five minutes. They also solve word problems involving dollar bills, quarters, dimes, nickels, and pennies.

Measurement data is used to pose questions, collect, analyze, represent data, and interpret results. *Second graders* learn to create line plots, picture graphs, and bar graphs to represent data with up to four categories. In turn, they solve problems using information in given bar graphs, as well as from graphs they create.

Geometry

Geometry topics permeate throughout elementary-, middle-, and high-school-grade levels because this big math idea is so much more than recalling the names of shapes, measuring angles, and making shape patterns. Children progress from studying shapes and related characteristics in the early grades to working with geometric proofs in high school.

Children's understanding of geometry concepts positions them to interpret and describe the physical environment. They learn to physically and mentally change the positions of objects, describe shapes and the relationships among them, as well as solve problems using spatial reasoning.

In *kindergarten*, children move from using informal to formal language to describe and name shapes. For example, descriptions such as "shaped like a basketball" become "a sphere." They begin to focus on geometric attributes to identify and describe two-dimensional shapes drawn in multiple ways (different sizes and positions), as well as three-dimensional shapes.

Kindergarteners use basic shapes and spatial reasoning to model objects in their environment. Children analyze and compare two- and three-dimensional shapes. They use simple shapes to form larger, more complex shapes by rotating, flipping, and arranging shapes and other objects such as puzzles, blocks, and everyday items. Through such exploration, they begin to understand that certain attributes define what a shape is, while other attributes do not.

Geometry is closely linked to other big ideas in math such as fractions and area. *First graders* start to recognize these links when they learn how "parts" are related to "wholes" while partitioning regions into equal pieces using words such as halves, thirds, and quarters of. Such understanding provides the foundations for more in-depth studies of fractions in later elementary grades. *First graders* are guided to label terms and use such terminology appropriately. Doing so supports children in developing the precision necessary for recognizing and describing similarities and differences among shapes.

Second graders start developing understanding about congruence (equal size), similarity (same shape, but not necessarily same size), and symmetry (balance). They recognize and draw shapes having specified attributes such as a given number of sides, angles, or equal faces. *Second graders* identify *triangles* (three-sided shapes), *quadrilaterals* (four-sided shapes), *pentagons* (five-sided shapes), *hexagons* (six-sided shapes), and *cubes* (solid shapes with six equally sized square faces).

Second graders also learn how to partition rectangles into equal-sized rows and columns and answer questions such as, "How many ways can a square be partitioned into thirds?" They partition circles and rectangles into two, three, and four equal regions. In addition, they describe shapes using terms such as halves, thirds, half of, and a fourth of. Wholes are described as two halves, three thirds, or four fourths.

CLASSROOM SCENES

The classroom scenes shared in this section are adapted from those presented in the book *Hands-On Standards* (published by ETA hand2mind) and represent a sampling of what learning looks like in today's Grades K–2 math classrooms. Examples are presented, classroom action steps outlined, and ways by which parents can provide related support at home described. You can access paper materials and student pages reflective of those shared at http://www.hand2mind.com/hosstudent.

Counting and Cardinality

Kindergarten Scene

This example demonstrates counting on.

Example: Christina's class is playing a game with a giant number line. The students start at number 0. A classmate tells them how many numbers to jump. They jump and then tell where they landed. Nicholas told Christina to jump 7 numbers. Where did Christina land?

Classroom Action Steps:

- Children are given a number line and a counter to represent jumping on a number line. After the example is read, children place a counter on number 0 on the number line. Then they show how the counter moves seven numbers. Children count as the counter moves.
- Children are asked:
  ○ Where did your counter land after moving 7 numbers?
- Next children place a counter at 1 on the number line. Then children show how the counter moves 7 numbers. Children count as the counter moves.
- Children are asked:
  ○ Where did your counter land after moving 7 numbers from number 1?

Figure 3.1 (Grade K—Counting and Cardinality). *Source:* Regina M. Mistretta

Parents Can:

You can reinforce this example at home with all different numbers for your child to start from and move. Draw a number line on paper and use a counter such as a checker or coin.

It's helpful to give your child experience moving numbers from different starting points. Sometimes children may start a counter on number 1 regardless of instructions because they are used to counting from one. You can help your child by reminding him or her to start the counter on the number you say and begin counting from that number.

Operations and Algebraic Thinking

Kindergarten Scene

This example is about making 10.

Example: Charlie has 6 toy trains in his case. The case can hold 10 toy trains. How many more toy trains can Charlie put in his case?

Classroom Action Steps:

- Children are given a ten-frame, along with counters.
- Explained to children is that the ten-frame will be used to show Charlie's toy trains in his case.

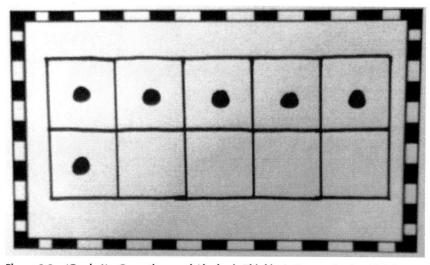

Figure 3.2   (Grade K—Operations and Algebraic Thinking). *Source:* Regina M. Mistretta

Example: Nicholas and Christina are bringing cookies to the class party. Nicholas is bringing 6 boxes of chocolate chip cookies. Christina is bringing 9 boxes of oatmeal cookies. How many boxes are they bringing in all?

Classroom Action Steps:

- Children are given ten-frames to represent the 6 boxes of chocolate chip cookies and the 9 boxes of oatmeal cookies as dots.
- Children are asked:
  ○ What do we have to find out?

The response elicited from children is that one needs to find out the total number of boxes. In turn, children join the dots in the two ten-frames to represent the sum, or total.

- Children then write about how they added (joined) all the dots (boxes) together.
- Children are asked:
  ○ Where did the four dots added to the top ten-frame come from?

The response elicited from children is that the four added dots came from breaking 9 into 4 and 5 and moving 4 up. They are then assisted in writing number sentences that represent this breakup of 9 into 4 and 5. They then add by making a 10 and adding on 5 more.

- Children are asked:
  ○ Which is easier to calculate in your head, $10 + 5$ or $6 + 9$?

The response elicited from children is that adding from 10 makes addition easier.

Parents Can:
Now, you may be thinking that this is an awful lot of work. Why not just memorize the fact? The thinking strategies used by your child help to develop deeply his or her sense of number relationships. Such deep foundational understanding will position him or her to develop computational fluency with meaning.

In other words, the answers your child computes will make sense because he or she is equipped with understanding about number relationships, rather than only memorized facts. So reinforcing at home similar examples can be extremely helpful to him or her. When representing your examples, use ten-frames with dots, color or paper tiles, snap cubes, or legos.

Second Grade Scene

This example is about addition and subtraction number sentences.

Example: Of the 17 students in our class, 8 students have pets. How many students do not have pets?

Classroom Action Steps:

• Reflecting the process of making 10 from the previous classroom scene, children use ten-frames to represent 17 as 10 and 7.
• To compute the involved subtraction example (17 – 8), children are guided to think about how to subtract down to 10 as a way of making the computation easier. Addition is the opposite of subtraction (known as inverse operations). So children's knowledge of addition supports success with this subtraction example.
• First, children are guided to break 8 into 7 and 1 in a way that they can subtract 7 from 17 in order to get to 10. At this point, children take 1 more away and arrive at the answer of 9.
• Children are then guided to represent their thinking in writing.

Parents Can:
You can reinforce this example at home by doing similar ones. Practice will help your child understand how addition facts can support subtraction computations.

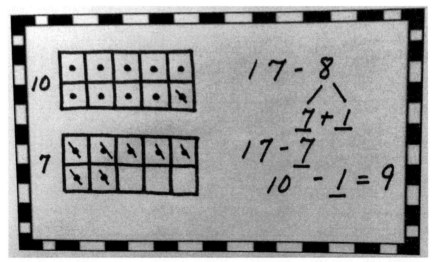

Figure 3.4   (Grade 2—Operations and Algebraic Thinking). *Source:* Regina M. Mistretta

Number and Operations in Base Ten

Kindergarten Scene

This example is about composing numbers 11 to 19.

Example: Jacob has 10 gingerbread dog biscuits and 3 bacon dog biscuits. How many dog biscuits does Jacob have in all?

Classroom Action Steps:

• Children are given ten-frames, as with the previous classroom scenes, to represent the dog biscuits in this example with dots.
• Children are asked:
  ○ How many gingerbread dog biscuits does Jacob have?
  Children represent the 10 biscuits on the ten-frame and are asked:
  ○ How many bacon dog biscuits does Jacob have?
  Children represent these biscuits on another ten-frame and are asked:
  ○ How can we find out how many dog biscuits Jacob has in all?
  The response elicited from children is that one needs to join the 3 dots with the 10 dots and count them all. They join the dots and write the addition sentence 10 + 3 = 13.

Parents Can:
Doing more of this type of example with your child reflects the type of engagement that initiates his or her understanding of place value. Practice similar examples that involve composing numbers from 10.

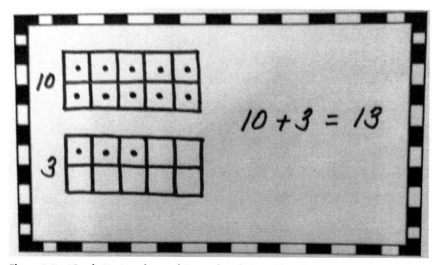

Figure 3.5   (Grade K—Number and Operations in Base Ten). *Source:* Regina M. Mistretta

First Grade Scene

This example is about working with place value.

Example: Charlie has 12 golf balls in a big blue bucket. His friend Nick didn't know Charlie had so many golf balls, so he went to the store and bought 7 golf balls so he could play golf with Charlie. When he added his 7 golf balls to Charlie's bucket, how many golf balls did they have in all? In how many different ways can you show this number?

Classroom Action Steps:

- Children are given base ten materials and a place value chart.
- Using ones (or units as they are sometimes called), children first make a group of 12 ones to represent Charlie's 12 golf balls. Children then make a group of 7 ones to represent Nick's golf balls. Explained to children is that counting all the ones is just one way to find, and show how many golf balls are there in all. Another way to show the total is then explored with children.
- Children look at a ten (or a rod as it is sometimes called) and are guided to see that it has 10 ones in it. Children count the 10 ones in the ten to confirm that the ten is the same amount as 10 ones.
- Explained to children is that a ten rod is called a "ten" since it has 10 ones in it.

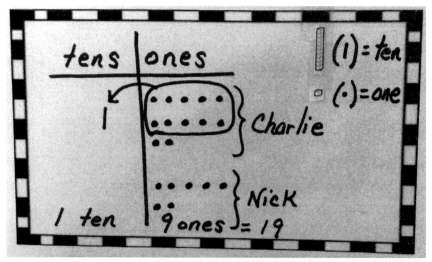

Figure 3.6   (Grade 1—Number and Operations in Base Ten). *Source:* Regina M. Mistretta

- Children then exchange 10 of the 19 ones on the place value chart for 1 ten and place it in the tens column.
- Pointed out to children is that the "1" in 19 is in the tens place and has a value of 10.
- Children are asked:
  ○ How many tens are in 19?
  ○ How many more ones are there in the ones column of the chart?
  ○ How many ones are in 19?

Parents Can:

You can reinforce this example at home by doing similar examples that engage your child in exchanging ones for a ten. A fun game you can play with your child is the exchange game. Gather a die and chips of two different colors. Take turns rolling the die and picking up that number of same color chips. Once you collect 10 chips, exchange them for another color chip, and you are the winner!

Second Grade Scene

This example is about place value with three-digit numbers.

Example: Charlie collects baseball cards. He had 97 baseball cards. Then his grandmother bought him another pack of 10 cards. How many baseball cards does Charlie have now?

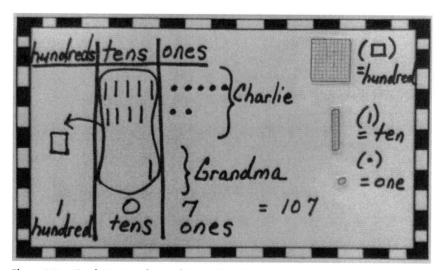

Figure 3.7 (Grade 2—Number and Operations in Base Ten). *Source:* Regina M. Mistretta

Classroom Action Steps:

- Children are given base ten materials and a place value chart.
- Children are asked:
  - How many baseball cards does Charlie have?
  - How can you show 97 using base ten blocks?
  - How many tens are in 97?
  - How many ones are in 97?
- Children count out 9 tens and 7 ones and place them in the tens and ones columns on the chart.
- Children are asked:
  - How many baseball cards did Charlie's grandmother buy him?
  - What should you add to your blocks to show the new pack of 10?
  - How many tens do you have now?
- Children are guided to push their 10 tens together and compare them to a hundred (or flat as they are sometimes called).
- The response elicited from children is that 10 tens is the same amount as 100.
- Children then exchange 10 tens for 100 and place the hundred in the hundreds column of the chart.
- Children are asked:
  - How many hundreds do you have?
  - How many tens do you have?
  - How many ones do you have?
- Children are told that this number can be written as 1 hundred, 0 tens, and 7 ones.

Parents Can:
You can reinforce this example at home by doing similar examples that engage your child in exchanging tens for a hundred. Doing additional examples such as this one with your child supports his or her understanding of computational procedures.

You can also extend the exchange game, explained in the previous classroom scene, to rolling the die and collecting another 10 chips to exchange for another color. The first person to attain that other color chip is the winner! You are readying your child to add, subtract, multiply, and divide in later grades with understanding of why the procedures make sense because of these early concrete experiences.

If your child isn't making the connection between the sizes of the base ten blocks and the place value positions in the numbers, remind him or her that the bigger blocks go on the left and the smaller blocks go on the right. The blocks get smaller going to the right, just like the numbers get smaller when you read them from left to right.

Measurement and Data

Kindergarten Scene

This example is about sorting objects by length.

Example: Christina drew a picture of four caterpillars crawling on the ground. She showed the picture to her parent. Her parent said that the worms were in order from shortest to longest. How can you show the order of the caterpillars in Christina's picture?

Classroom Action Steps:

- Children are shown representations of the caterpillars with snap cubes.
- Children count the number of cubes in each of the caterpillars and line them up on the left-hand sides. A straight edge is sometimes used to help align the caterpillars.
- Children then rearrange the caterpillars from shortest to longest, with the shortest caterpillar on top.

Parents Can:
Doing additional examples reflective of the one above reinforces your child's understanding of length. Use snap cubes or legos in a way that the pieces stay together and your child can focus on the lengths. If your child does not align the caterpillars on the left sides, model the correct alignment for him or her.

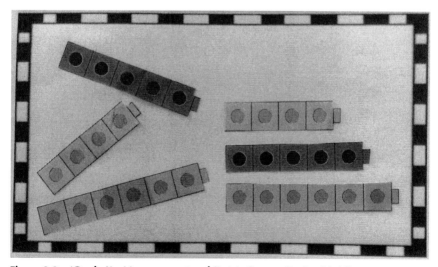

Figure 3.8 (Grade K—Measurement and Data). *Source*: Regina M. Mistretta

It's helpful to give your child a ruler or other straightedge to help align the lengths. Also, make sure he or she does not confuse *longest* with *tallest*. Remind him or her that *tallest* describes direction from the ground. Length is measured left to right, or side to side.

First Grade Scene

This example is about making a histogram.

Example: Your class can get one new color of construction paper: green, blue, or orange to use for art projects. Which color is the favorite of most children in your class?

Classroom Action Steps:

- Children are surveyed to determine how many children prefer each color. Tally marks are used to show the survey results.
- Explained to children is that a graph is a picture that shows data, and they will make a histogram about the class data to help see which color most children in the class prefer.
- Children are given a graphing grid and guided in labeling three rows at the left side of the grid with the names of the three colors.
- Children then number each row at the bottom of the graph, beginning with 1 and counting over by ones to 8.

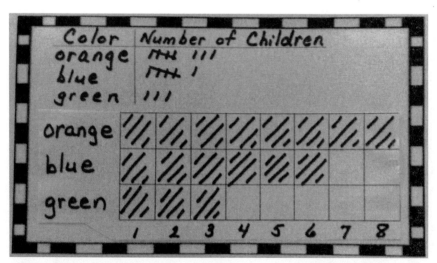

Figure 3.9   (Grade 1—Measurement and Data). *Source:* Regina M. Mistretta

- Children transfer the tally mark data onto the graph by shading one square on the graph to represent each tally mark.
- Discussion is then facilitated with children about how the graph helps answer the question initially posed.

Parents Can:

Doing additional examples reflective of the one above reinforces your child's ability to collect and represent data on a bar graph. Please note that the graph shown for this classroom scene is a histogram because the bars are connected. A bar graph is one where the bars are actually separated from each other. Survey other information about your family. Record the data with tally marks and craft a histogram, as well as a bar graph.

If your child is not representing the correct number in each bar on the graph, have him or her count out the correct number of squares first. He or she can then shade them on the graph using one-to-one correspondence.

Second Grade Scene

This is an example about representing whole numbers as lengths.

Example: Sam took a marker and moved it from 3 cm on his number line to 7 cm. Then Sam moved his marker forward 5 cm. Where did Sam's marker land? Write a number sentence to show the distance that Sam's marker moved on the number line.

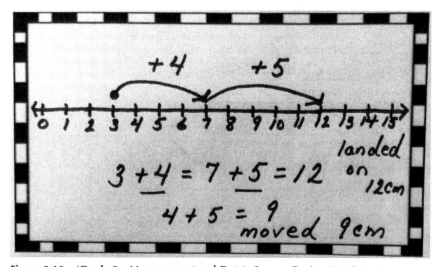

Figure 3.10 (Grade 2—Measurement and Data). *Source:* Regina M. Mistretta

Classroom Action Steps:

- Children use a centimeter number line to show Sam moving his marker.
- Children are asked:
  ○ Where should you start on the number line?
  ○ What does Sam do next?
- Children are guided to show the marker moving forward five spaces.
  ○ Where is Sam's marker now?
- Explained to children is that they can write about the movement on the number line with number sentences. The number sentences written are 3 + 4 = 7 and 7 + 5 = 12.
- Discussion is facilitated with children about how a total of 9 cm were moved and the marker landed on 12 cm.

Parents Can:
Doing additional examples reflective of the one above reinforces your child's understanding of number sentences. Watch that he or she counts accurately on the number line and starts at the appropriate place.

Geometry

Kindergarten Scene

This is an example about geometric pictures and designs.

Example: Mrs. Mistretta's class is making tangram designs with seven shapes: two large triangles, one medium triangle, two small triangles, a square, and a parallelogram. Find the tangram pieces in the design made by one of Mrs. Mistretta's students.

Classroom Action Steps:

- Children are given a set of tangram pieces and an outline of a design.
- Children explore the tangram pieces and review their names and sizes. They then begin to look for the tangram pieces in the design.
- Children find each tangram piece in the design, and they are asked about how many sides and how many corners are in each of the pieces.

Parents Can:
Using additional picture outlines with your child in a similar manner as described above helps reinforce his or her understanding of the attributes of specific shapes. Tangram pieces and additional picture outlines can be found at http://www.activityvillage.co.uk/tangrams. The solutions are available at the site as well so that you can print the picture and fill in the outlines of the pieces.

Figure 3.11 (Grade K—Geometry). *Source*: Regina M. Mistretta

You can also use tangrams online at http://illuminations.nctm.org/Activity. aspx?id=6384.

If your child is struggling to find shapes in the pictures, hold up the individual tangram pieces in various positions and have him or her review with you each piece's attributes. For example, remind him or her that a square has four sides that are all of the same length. Then ask him or her to see if they can find a shape in the picture that has four sides that are all of the same length.

First Grade Scene

This is an example about combining shapes to compose new shapes.

Example: Mr. Oliver's class is making shapes using tangram pieces. He asks his class to make a square, a triangle, and a parallelogram. How can these shapes be made using tangram pieces?

Classroom Action Steps:

• Children are given a set of tangrams as shown above in the kindergarten scene. Each of the pieces is reviewed with particular attention given to the parallelogram. This piece may be unfamiliar to children at this grade level.
• Children are then asked to make a square with other tangram pieces.
• For each child's solutions, he or she is asked to trace the shapes onto paper as a means of recording solutions.

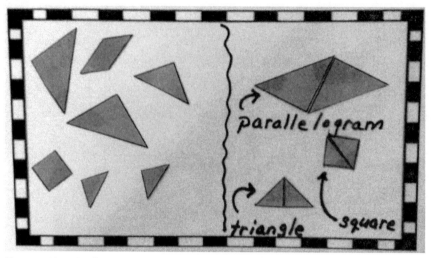

Figure 3.12 (Grade 1—Geometry). *Source:* Regina M. Mistretta

- The previous two steps are repeated for the parallelogram, as well as for a triangle.
- Discussion is facilitated about how the solutions are similar and different. This also includes where the shapes can be found in the real world such as the classroom, playground, home, and so on.

Parents Can:

Building shapes with tangrams in ways similar to those above supports your child's spatial understanding. If he or she is struggling to see how tangram pieces fit together to make other shapes, you can help him or her by drawing on a piece of paper the shape you asked him or her to build. Then draw a line to show the shadow of one smaller shape within it.

For example, if you ask your child to make a medium triangle, draw the medium triangle on a piece of paper. Then draw a line to show one of the small triangles that is within that medium triangle. Ask him or her if he or she can see another small triangle in the medium triangle.

Second Grade Scene

This is an example about partitioning rectangles.

Example: Rosemarie is making a paper place mat with different-colored square tiles. The place mat has 8 rows of square tiles with 10 squares in each row. All the square tiles are of the same size. How many square tiles are in the place mat?

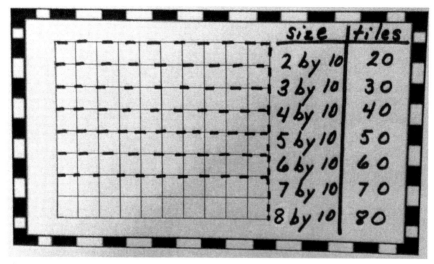

size	tiles
2 by 10	20
3 by 10	30
4 by 10	40
5 by 10	50
6 by 10	60
7 by 10	70
8 by 10	80

Figure 3.13 (Grade 2—Geometry). *Source*: Regina M. Mistretta

Classroom Action Steps:

- Children are given square-inch tiles they can color, along with an 8- by 10-inch piece of paper.
- Explained to children is the fact that rows run left to right and columns run top to down.
- Children are asked:
  ○ How many square tiles are in each row?
  Children then build the first row of the place mat by pasting tiles onto the paper.
- Children then build the second row to form a 2 by 10 rectangle.
  The response elicited from children as they build this additional row with equal-sized square tiles is that the rectangle gets larger.
- Children continue to make larger and larger rectangles and are asked along the way:
  ○ How many rows are in the place mat now?
  ○ How many square tiles have you used so far?
- Once the 8- by 10-inch piece of paper is completely covered, children are asked:
  ○ How many square tiles are in Rosemarie's place mat?

Parents Can:
This is a fun task you and your child can do at home. Making paper place mats for the kitchen table can support your child in visualizing the concept

of area as the amount of space getting covered while he or she creates the place mat.

Partitioning rectangles in this manner supports the development of multiplication skills as well since your child is working with a number of tiles that repeat over and over again. Visualizing this repeated amount supports your child's future learning of multiplication as a means for repeatedly adding a certain amount of equal-sized groups.

For example, the above place mat when complete has 80 square tiles in it, or 8 groups of 10 (8 × 10). Have fun at dinnertime engaging in conversation about the math in your place mats!

Chapter 4

Big Math Ideas in Grades 3–5

This chapter joins chapter 3 in providing descriptions about how big math ideas develop across the grades; this chapter focuses on Grades 3 through 5. A sampling of grade-level examples, entitled *Classroom Scenes*, provides an insider's view into how content unfolds in these grade-level classrooms. Coupled with these scenes are guidelines for parents about how to support such learning at home.

DEVELOPING CONTENT

Operations and Algebraic Thinking

In *third grade*, children develop understanding of the meanings of multiplication and division of whole numbers. Using prior knowledge about number relationships, they solve multiplication and division problems involving single-digit *factors* (numbers multiplied together), such as 8 × 5. In so doing, *third graders* use increasingly sophisticated strategies.

While comparing solution strategies, children learn about the relationship between multiplication and division. For example, they discover how multiplication can be thought of as repeated addition, while subtraction can be thought of as repeated subtraction. Also, they learn how multiplication involves joining a certain number of equal groups, while division separates quantities into equal groups. A goal for *third graders* is to understand and memorize all the *products* (answers to multiplication) of two one-digit numbers.

In *fourth grade*, children build on their understanding of addition, subtraction, multiplication, and division of whole numbers. They solve multistep word problems using these four operations. They reason about whether or not answers make sense, use estimation strategies, look for patterns, and make generalizations about the procedures they use to calculate answers.

Fourth graders also learn about prime and composite numbers. A *prime number* has exactly two factors (1 and itself). A *composite number* has more than two factors. For example, 3 is a prime number because only 1 × 3 equals 3, thus having only two factors. The number 4 is a composite number because 1, 2, and 4 can multiply together to equal 4; thus having more than two factors (1 × 4, 2 × 2).

In addition, *fourth graders* learn about algebraic concepts and related applications. For example, they generate outputs based on a given rule, such as "add 4," and identify patterns in the *outputs* (results or answers). Such work readies them for learning about functions and equations in higher grade levels.

Fifth graders further develop their fluency with addition and subtraction of whole numbers and learn how to multiply and divide fractions. These children develop skills in writing and interpreting numerical expressions that include grouping symbols. Such work supports their use of the order of operations. *Order of operations* means the sequencing of computations. Specifically, computations within parentheses are completed first; then, exponents, multiplications and divisions; and finally, additions and subtractions.

Fifth graders also use algebraic thinking skills to analyze patterns and relationships. While *fourth graders* generate numerical patterns using one rule, *fifth graders* generate patterns using two rules, such as "add 4, multiply by 2."

Number and Operations in Base Ten

The base ten number system, or "place value" system, determines the value of numerals based on their position. For example, 6 in 16 has a value of 6 ones, whereas 6 in 61 has a value of 6 tens or 60. *Third graders* continue developing the place value understanding from Grades kindergarten to 2. They explain and reason about answers when *rounding* (estimating) and performing multidigit arithmetic.

Third graders apply their understanding of place value and procedures, referred to as *algorithms*, to fluently add and subtract numbers up to 1000. *Fluency* means applying accuracy, efficiency, and flexibility. Efficiency involves using a reasonable number of steps in an appropriate amount of time when solving math problems. Flexibility involves adjusting a problem-solving strategy to suit the math situation.

In *fourth grade*, children are guided to generalize their understanding of place value to 1,000,000. They come to recognize that in multidigit whole numbers, a digit in one place represents 10 times what it represents in the place to its right. For example, the second 6 in 661 has a value of 60, while the first 6 in 661 has a value of 600, or 10 times 60.

Fourth graders read and write multidigit whole numbers using base ten numerals such as 123, number names such as one hundred and twenty-three, and expanded form such as (100 + 20 + 3). These children compare two multidigit numbers based on the meaning of the digits in each place using symbols such as > (greater than), = (equal to), and < (less than). In addition, *fourth graders* use their understanding of place value to round multidigit whole numbers to any place.

Fourth grade involves children applying their understanding of models for multiplication and division. They develop fluency with procedures for multiplying whole numbers, and they come to understand that dividing numbers is the opposite of multiplying them. For example, children are guided to understand that the multiplication fact $6 \times 3 = 18$ means joining (or repeatedly adding) 6 groups of 3 items for a total of 18 items. They are also guided to understand that $18 \div 3 = 6$ means separating (or repeatedly subtracting) groups of 3 items from 18 to arrive at an answer of 6 groups of 3 items (or subtracting 3 six times).

In addition, *fourth graders* develop generalizable procedures for finding quotients to division problems involving multidigit dividends. *Quotient* is the answer to a division problem. *Dividend* is the number being divided. *Divisor* is the number of groupings being formed or subtracted away from the dividend. For example, in $16 \div 8 = 2$, the number 2 is the quotient and the number 16 is the divisor. The number 8 is the *dividend*, or number of items being grouped together, or the number of groups being formed, or the number being repeatedly subtracted from 16.

In *fifth grade*, children extend their learning to understand base ten relationships among decimals. They come to understand that in a multidigit number, a digit in one place represents 1/10 of what it represents in the place to its left. For example, the first 6 in 166 has a value of 60, while the second 6 in 166 has a value of 6 (or 1/10 of 60).

Fifth graders develop fluency with adding and subtracting decimals. They learn why the division procedures they learned in previous grades make sense with decimals, and how to place the decimal point when multiplying or dividing a decimal number by a power of 10 (10, 100, 1000, etc.). In addition, these children read, write, and compare decimals to thousandths and use place value understanding to round decimals to any place.

Number and Operations—Fractions

Children in *third grade* develop an understanding of fractions as fair sharing, parts of a whole, and parts of a set. They use fractions to represent numbers less than, equal to, and greater than 1. They also solve problems that involve comparing fractions by using concrete visual aids and strategies stemming from their observations of equal numerators and denominators.

Numerator is the top number of a fraction that represents an amount of equal part(s) of a whole. *Denominator* is the bottom number of a fraction that represents the total amount of equal parts in the whole. For example, in ¾ the numerator is 3 and represents 3 equal parts of a whole, while the denominator is 4 and represents the whole divided into 4 equal parts. So, ¾ represents 3 out of the 4 equal parts of a whole.

In *third grade*, children work for the first time with a number line to represent numbers between whole numbers. They are guided to explain equivalence of fractions and compare fractions by reasoning about their sizes. *Third graders*, through the use of concrete materials and visual aids, come to understand *equivalent fractions* as fractions representing the same size or lying at the same point on a number line. For example, ½ is equivalent to 2/4.

A substantial amount of *fourth grade* involves exploring fractions. Children compare fractions with common denominators and numerators. They record and justify their answers with the symbols <, =, and >. They focus on *unit fractions*, meaning those fractions that have a numerator of 1.

In addition, *fourth graders* learn how to add and subtract mixed numbers with like denominators by replacing each mixed number with an equivalent fraction. *Mixed number* means a whole number and a fraction such as 4 ½. *Fourth graders* also explore the idea that numbers can be represented as both fractions and decimals. They learn how to convert fractions to decimals and compare decimal fractions such as 3/10 and 6/100 (0.3 and 0.06).

In *fifth grade*, children learn how to add and subtract fractions with unlike denominators and solve related word problems. They use benchmark fractions such as ½, and ¼, and their fraction number sense to assess the reasonableness of answers. *Fifth graders* also use their number sense to jockey between decimal and fraction equivalents.

Fifth graders extend their previous learning of multiplication and division to multiply two fractions together, as well as a whole number and a fraction together. They move beyond thinking about multiplication as repeated addition to also understanding multiplication as *scaling* or resizing.

As part of their developing understanding, *fifth graders* learn that fractions also represent the division of two quantities. For example, ¾ means 3 divided by 4. They divide unit fractions by whole numbers and whole numbers by unit fractions while solving real-world problems. In addition, *fifth graders* understand and explain why the procedures for multiplying and dividing fractions make sense.

Measurement and Data

Third grade involves several concepts related to measurement and data. Children measure concrete objects with traditional rulers and "measure" time by telling and writing time to the nearest minute, as well as solving problems relating to elapsed time.

Third graders develop foundational understanding of *partitioning* (subdividing units of measure), *iteration* (repeating units of measure), and *compensation* (size of the unit of measure that determines the number of units needed). These children learn how to measure *area* (how much space an object covers) by using square units, and they develop understanding of *perimeter* as the distance around a flat object.

Third graders also learn how to measure *volume*, meaning the amount of space taken up by a three-dimensional object. They use standard rulers with half and quarter markings to measure lengths. They use the knowledge of fractions they received in previous grades to measure objects to the nearest one-half and one-quarter inch. In addition, these children show data by making line plots with a horizontal scale marked off in whole numbers, halves, and quarters.

Reading and solving problems using scaled graphs, such as picture and bar graphs, is also part of learning math in *third grade*. Children solve one-step and two-step "how many more" and "how many less" problems while using information from graphs they read. While exploring data, they pose their own questions, along with collecting, analyzing, and interpreting data relevant to everyday life.

Fourth graders learn how the sizes of measurement units within a measurement system are related. For example, these children come to understand that 100 cm equal a meter and that 1000 meters equal a kilometer.

Fourth graders solve multistep word problems involving distances, time intervals, liquid volume, and money. They use diagrams that include measurement scales, such as number lines, to represent quantities. They learn how to apply formulas of area and perimeter while solving real-world math problems. In addition, they represent and interpret data pertaining to objects they measure and craft line plots to display data and solve related problems.

Fourth graders come to recognize *angles* as geometric shapes formed when two rays share a common endpoint. *Ray* is a line with one endpoint that extends *infinitely* (forever) in one direction. They learn that angles can be divided into a sum of smaller angles, in turn applying this knowledge when asked to find unknown angles. They also use protractors to determine angle measurements and draw angles to given degree sizes.

Fifth graders learn how to convert units within a given measurement system (such as converting feet into inches) and use those converted units to solve multistep problems. While computing conversions, they come to recognize existing connections between the base ten number system and the metric measurement system.

Fifth grade also involves making line plots to display data involving fractions, as well as adding and subtracting fraction data on line plots to solve problems involving length, mass, and volume. In addition, *fifth graders* come to understand how volume is measured by finding the total number of *unit cubes* (cubes with sides of length 1) needed to exactly fill a space. They are guided to choose appropriate units, strategies, and tools for solving problems that involve estimating and measuring volume.

Geometry

Third graders are engaged in describing, analyzing, and comparing properties of two-dimensional shapes. They define shapes by comparing and classifying them according to their sides and angles. For example, children recognize that rhombii, squares, and rectangles have four sides, and therefore they are all classified as *quadrilaterals*. They are also guided to note characteristics of angles and relationships between opposite sides in quadrilaterals.

Third graders relate their fraction knowledge to geometry. They partition shapes into halves, thirds, fourths, sixths, and eighths. Using such fractions, they express the area of part of a shape as a fraction of a whole in multiple ways.

Fourth graders draw points, lines, and angles. To deepen their understanding of two-dimensional shapes, children are guided to focus on the classifications of shapes and symmetry. *Symmetry* means the proportion or balance that can exist within shapes.

Fourth graders learn about *parallel* lines (lines that run side by side and never cross) and *perpendicular* lines (lines that cross and form 90-degree angles), along with *right, acute, and obtuse angles*. Right angles measure 90 degrees; acute angles measure less than 90 degrees; and obtuse angles measure more than 90 degrees but less than 180 degrees.

In *fourth grade*, children also learn about right triangles as triangles having one 90-degree angle. They come to recognize *right triangles* as one category of triangle and are guided to identify different types of right triangles according to lengths of existing sides.

Fifth grade children are introduced to the *coordinate plane*, a space consisting of points located on an xy axes. The *x-axis* is the horizontal line, while the *y-axis* is the vertical line of a coordinate plane. *Fifth graders* plot points using (x,y) coordinates where x and y are both positive numbers. The *x-coordinate* is a number on the x-axis, and the *y-coordinate* is a number on the y-axis.

Fifth graders also develop more sophisticated classification skills concerning two-dimensional shapes. For example, given that all rectangles have four right angles, and that squares are special types of *rectangles* (opposite sides are equal), children conclude that all squares have four right angles.

CLASSROOM SCENES

The classroom scenes shared in this section are adapted from those included in the book *Hands-On Standards* (published by ETA hand2mind) and represent a sampling of what learning looks like in today's Grades 3 through 5 math classrooms. Examples are presented, classroom action steps outlined, and ways parents can provide related support at home described. You can access paper materials and student pages reflective of those shared at http://www.hand2mind.com/hosstudent.

Operations and Algebraic Thinking

Third Grade Scene

This example is about relating arrays and repeated addition to multiplication.

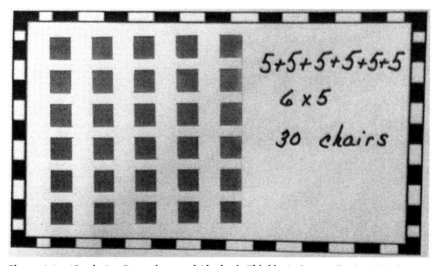

Figure 4.1 (Grade 3—Operations and Algebraic Thinking). *Source*: Regina M. Mistretta

Example: Mr. Mistretta asked a parent to speak to his class about how they use math at their job in the hospital for Career Awareness Week. Mr. Mistretta invited the other third grade class to come and listen as well. Mr. Mistretta made room for all the students in his classroom by arranging chairs into 6 rows, and put 5 chairs in each row. How many chairs were in the classroom in all?

Classroom Action Steps:

- Children are given tiles and told that one way to solve the problem is by using an array. An *array* is an arrangement of equal groups that can be used to represent repeated addition (multiplication).
  Children are then instructed to use the tiles to show 6 rows of 5 tiles.
- Children are asked:
  ○ How can you find the total number of tiles in the array?
  Pointed out to children is that they can use the array to add
  $5 + 5 + 5 + 5 + 5 + 5$.
- Children then calculate the answer by adding, and are asked:
  ○ Are there other ways that you can find the answer?
  Discussed with children is that 6×5 is the same as $5 + 5 + 5 + 5 + 5 + 5$. In other words, 6×5 means 6 groups of 5 tiles, or $5 + 5 + 5 + 5 + 5 + 5$.

Parents Can:
You can reinforce this example at home by modeling similar examples with tiles or other objects you have at home. Make sure your child understands the difference between a row and a column. Also, if your child doesn't understand that he or she needs to have the same number of tiles in each row, discuss that in order to represent repeated addition for multiplication one needs the same number in each group.

In addition, encourage your child to use skip counting for repeated addition before memorizing multiplication facts. This will give your child a deeper understanding of what multiplication is, rather than merely memorizing facts.

Fourth Grade Scene

This example is about identifying pattern rules.

Example: Mrs. Mistretta and her students are planting a flower garden in front of their school. She and the class decide to plant 3 red geraniums in the first section, 6 in the second section, and 9 in the third section. What is the rule for the pattern? Can you find how many flower plants she and her students will plant in the twelfth section?

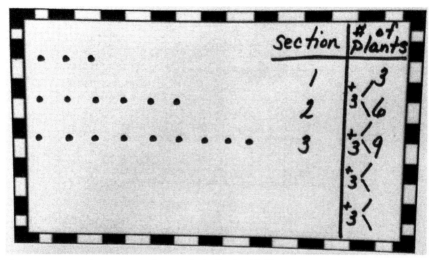

Figure 4.2   (Grade 4—Operations and Algebraic Thinking). *Source:* Regina M. Mistretta

Classroom Action Steps:

• Children use dots to show the pattern 3, 6, and 9 plants in sections 1, 2, and 3.
• Children are then asked to describe the pattern to their classmates. For this example, they are guided to recognize that each group of dots has three more dots than the previous group.
• Children are informed that they can now use their discovered rule to predict what comes next in the pattern. They then predict the next amounts in the pattern.

Parents Can:
Looking for patterns in similar ways supports your child in acquiring a skill that is basic to algebra. He or she may be confused by patterns that go down in size if he or she is only seeing patterns that go up in size. So, write out the pattern 19, 17, 15, 13, 11, 9, 7, 5, 3, 1. Use dots to represent the pattern and show your child the visual decline in the pattern that corresponds to the numerical values.

Fifth Grade Scene

This example is about the order of operations.

Example: Jacob brought some water bottles to the park to share with his playmates. He had 4 single water bottles and 3 multipacks. There are 5 water bottles in each multipack. To determine how many water bottles Jacob brought to the park, evaluate $4 + 3 \times 5$.

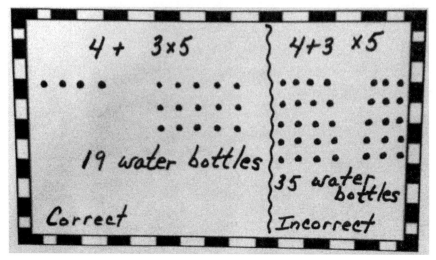

Figure 4.3 (Grade 5—Operations and Algebraic Thinking). *Source*: Regina M. Mistretta

Classroom Action Steps:

- Children use dots to represent water bottles and model the example. They are guided to start by drawing 4 dots. They then add a 3-by-5 array, and are asked how many dots are shown in the illustration.
- Next, children are asked to show 4 + 3 with dots. They are guided to draw an array to show this quantity (4 + 3) multiplied by 5 and are then asked how many dots are shown in this model.
- Children compare the two models and describe how the models differ, as well as which one is correct and why.
  The first model is the accurate one because it shows 3 multipacks of 5 bottles each, whereas the second model does not.
- Explained to children is that the *order of operations* provides rules for arriving at the correct example as shown in their drawing. The rules discussed with children are as follows:
  ○ Do computations inside parentheses first.
  ○ Then do computations involving exponents.
  ○ Next, multiply or divide from left to right.
  ○ Finally, add or subtract from left to right.

Parents Can:
You can reinforce this example at home by doing similar examples with dots. Because we read English from left to right, your child may continue to simplify expressions by performing operations in that order. If so, have him or

her write the order of operations at the top of his or her paper as a reference. A common mnemonic used to remember these rules is *P*lease *E*xcuse *M*y *D*ear *A*unt *S*ally (*P*arentheses, *E*xponents, *M*ultiplications/*D*ivisions, *A*dditions/*S*ubtractions).

Number and Operations in Base Ten

Third Grade Scene

This example is about adding and subtracting.

Example: Draw and solve: 189 + 219 – 85

Classroom Action Steps:

- Children are given base ten materials and a place value chart to model the example. Using ones (sometimes referred to as units), tens (sometimes referred to as rods), and hundreds (sometimes referred to as flats), children model 189 and 219.
- Children join the blocks together to model addition; regrouping occurs by exchanging a group of 10 ones for a ten, and a group of 10 tens for a hundred.

  This concrete experience develops children's understanding of the symbolic procedure used when adding with regrouping. A term you yourself may have used as a student is "carry over." The current term, "regrouping," is used to better define for children the action that is occurring while adding.

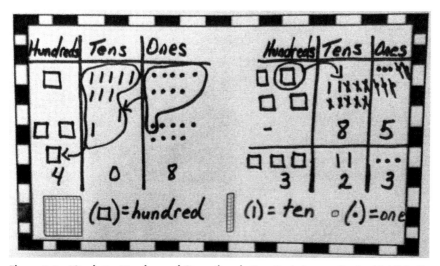

Figure 4.4 (Grade 3—Number and Operations in Base Ten). *Source*: Regina M. Mistretta

- Children are then assisted in taking their answer and representing it on a second place value chart where subtraction is performed. Here again, regrouping takes place in order to do the subtraction. The exchange of a hundred for 10 tens takes place so that 8 tens can be subtracted (shown through cross-outs).

Parents Can:

Doing more of this type of example with your child reflects the type of engagement that reinforces his or her understanding of place value while adding and subtracting.

Fourth Grade Scene

This example is about multiplying with a one-digit multiplier.

Example: Draw and solve: 3 × 21

Classroom Action Steps:

- Children are given base ten materials and a place value chart.
- Using ones (sometimes referred to as units) and tens (sometimes referred to as rods), children make 3 groups of 21.
- Next, children are asked to find the total number represented by the base ten materials. They count all the materials and express the answer symbolically.

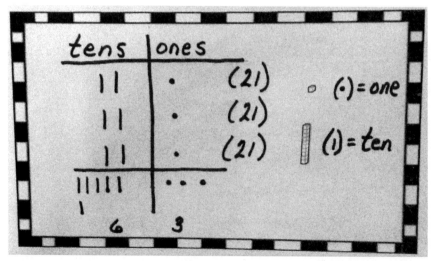

Figure 4.5   (Grade 4—Number and Operations in Base Ten). *Source:* Regina M. Mistretta

Parents Can:

You can reinforce this type of example at home by doing similar examples that engage your child in modeling multiplication. If he or she isn't grasping the concept of multiplication as repeated addition, explain to him or her the meanings behind the examples. More specifically, discuss and show how 3 × 21 means multiplying 21 three times, or adding 3 groups of 21.

Fifth Grade Scene

This is an example about adding and subtracting decimals.

Example: 0.7 + 0.5 − 0.3

Classroom Action Steps:

• Children are given base ten materials and a place value chart. This time the materials take on different meanings from when children used them for operations on *whole numbers* such as 7, rather than the *decimal* 0.7. A hundred (flat) is now considered a whole (1), the ten (rod) now represents a tenth (1/10) of it, and the one (unit) now represents a hundredth (1/100). These new names come from looking at the base ten materials differently. Since ten rods can cover a whole, one rod is considered 1 out of the ten, or 1/10, of the whole flat. Similarly, since 100 units can cover an entire flat, one unit is considered one hundredth, or 1/100, of the entire flat.

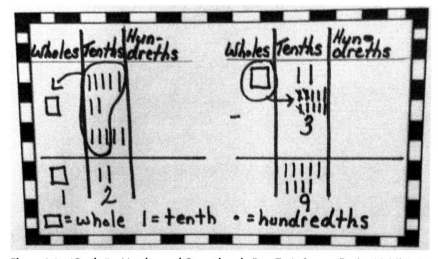

Figure 4.6 (Grade 5—Number and Operations in Base Ten). *Source*: Regina M. Mistretta

- Children model 0.7 and 0.5, and then join the materials together.
- From this total, children then subtract 0.3 and record the action with cross-outs.

Parents Can:

You can reinforce this type of example at home by doing similar examples that engage your child in using base ten materials to model addition and subtraction of decimals. If your child isn't grasping the new ways of thinking about the base ten materials, review with him or her how the new names came about. Stress that the hundred (flat) is now serving as 1 whole and that the other materials (rods and units) are parts of it.

Number and Operations—Fractions

Third Grade Scene

This is an example about equivalent fractions.

Example: Christina's family celebrated her birthday with a chocolate cake. Her mom cut the cake into 6 equal slices, and the family ate 4 of the 6 slices. What fraction of the cake was left over?

Classroom Action Steps:

- Fraction circles are given to children to assemble. In so doing, they discover how circles can be divided into different numbers and sizes of pieces.

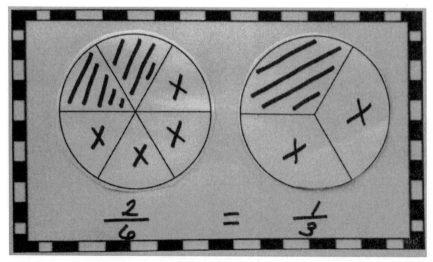

Figure 4.7   (Grade 3—Number and Operations—Fractions). *Source:* Regina M. Mistretta

- Children are asked to model the cake described in the above example with the fraction circles; these circles allow for 1 whole cake to be represented as 6 equal slices.
- Children are then asked to take away (indicated with x marks) the 4 cake slices the family ate and determine the fraction of the cake that is left.
- In addition, children are asked to determine another fraction name to represent the 2/6 of the cake that is left over. The purpose for this is that children can develop understanding for different fraction names that refer to the same amount of space. In other words, the goal here is for children to determine the *equivalent fractions* 2/6 and 1/3.

Parents Can:

Have your child create other equivalent fractions such as 1/2 and 2/4 using circle pieces. Stress that equivalent fractions are two different fraction names that represent the same amount of space.

Now, let's say your child puts together 1/3 and 1/6 to show 1/2. Although these two fractions added together equal 1/2, your child is not creating an equivalent fraction for 1/2. Rather, he or she has formed an addition sentence. So, reinforce the one-to-one correspondence of equivalent fractions and guide your child to represent 1/2 = 3/6 as two equivalent fractions.

Fourth Grade Scene

This is an example about adding and subtracting fractions.

Example: Christina's family celebrated her birthday with a chocolate cake. Her mom cut the cake into 6 equal slices. Christina ate 2/6 of the cake, and her brother ate 2/6 of it. What fraction of the cake was left for Christina's mom and dad to eat?

Classroom Action Steps:

- Fraction circles are given to children for them to model the fractional parts of the cake eaten by Christina and her brother.
- Children join the fractional parts together to show the total amount of cake eaten. Next, they are guided to write an addition sentence that represents the model.
- Children are then asked to determine a rule for adding fractions by looking at the model and its corresponding fraction names.
  Here is a situation where children are determining the computational procedure, rather than the teacher providing it to them. Children will better understand, and more likely retain, the procedure for adding fractions

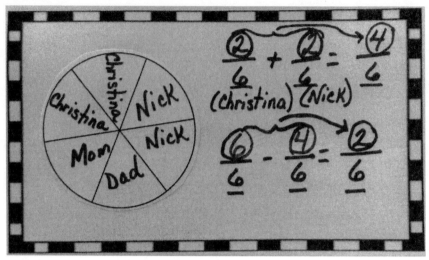

Figure 4.8 (Grade 4—Number and Operations—Fractions). *Source*: Regina M. Mistretta

(keeping the common denominator and adding the numerators) because they constructed the procedure.
- Next children determine what part of the cake is left for Christina's mom and dad to eat.

  Children are guided to find that 2/6 completes the whole, so the difference is 2/6.

  They write a number sentence to represent the model and again are asked to determine a rule, or procedure, this time for subtracting fractions.

For the same reasons as previously explained, children determine that to subtract fractions they keep the common denominator and subtract the numerators.

Parents Can:
You can reinforce the procedure for adding and subtracting fractions with like denominators by having your child model and record number sentences similar to the example described above.

Your child may want to express his or her answer in simpler form, such as 2/3 rather than 4/6. In such a case, explain to him or her that they are correct. However, for these types of examples, the goal is to master the rule for adding and subtracting fractions with like denominators. So, he or she should keep the denominator given in the example. Inform him or her that in future work with unlike denominators, he or she will use these other fraction names to complete computations.

Fifth Grade Scene

This is an example about using fractions as division.

Example: Three children need to share 4 muffins equally. How many muffins does each child get?

Classroom Action Steps:

- Children are given fraction circles and asked:
  ○ How many muffins are there?
- Children are asked to show the 4 muffins with 4 whole fraction circles or by tracing a whole fraction circle four times. Children are then asked:
  ○ How many children are there?
  ○ How would you write about this situation as a division problem?
  Such questioning elicits from children the example 4 ÷ 3.
- Children are asked the following questions to scaffold their thinking:
  ○ How can you divide those 4 circles evenly by 3?
  ○ If each child gets one whole muffin, how will they divide the remaining muffin?
  ○ What fraction of the remaining muffin will each child get?
- Explain to children that one can write this division example as the fraction 4/3. Next, children are asked:
  ○ What mixed number does the fraction 4/3 equal?

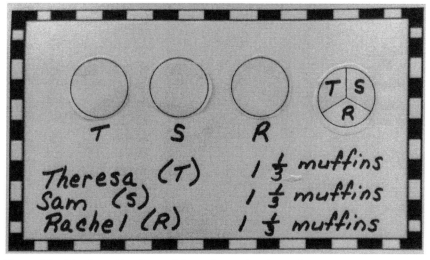

Figure 4.9   (Grade 5—Number and Operations—Fractions). *Source:* Regina M. Mistretta

Such modeling and questioning guide children to determine that each child gets 1 whole muffin and 1/3 of another muffin, or 1 1/3 muffins.

Parents Can:
You may be saying, "So many questions, why?" Well, through questioning, your child's thinking develops. This form of learning is much more powerful for your child than just mechanically doing or memorizing what others tell him or her. His or her math habits of mind develop by doing math in ways that make sense of it. In turn, he or she will become resourceful, rather than rely on others to tell him or her what to do.

Reinforce such thinking with additional examples reflective of the one explained above. Engage in conversation while having muffins for breakfast, or any other situation where a remaining whole will need to be shared evenly. If your child struggles with dividing the remaining whole, remind him or her to think about equal shares of that amount.

Measurement and Data

Third Grade Scene

This example is about finding the area of rectangles.

Example: For rainy days, Maya's mom wants to put square rug tiles on the pantry floor for everyone to wipe their feet when they come home. The pantry measures 8 units long by 6 units wide. Each rug tile measures 1 unit on each side. How many rug tiles will fill this area in the pantry?

Classroom Action Steps:

- Children represent tiles with squares on grid paper, and they are told that these squares will help find out how many tiles are needed to fill the pantry area that has sides of 8 and 6. A rectangle is drawn to represent the pantry area and terms defined. Specifically, they are told that *long* means from left to right and *wide* means from top to bottom.
- Children are then asked to make a rectangle that is 8 units long and 6 units wide. Next, children are asked how many tiles (squares) they used in total.
- This task continues for other rectangles with different dimensions such as 3 units long, 4 units wide; and 5 units long, 2 units wide.

Parents Can:
The goal of this activity is to further develop your child's understanding of *area* as the amount of space an object takes up. In addition, this scene sets the

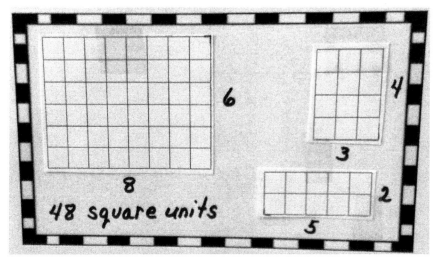

Figure 4.10 (Grade 3—Measurement and Data). *Source*: Regina M. Mistretta

groundwork for determining the area formula for a rectangle. Through concrete explorations and collection of data, your child is positioned to discover how he or she can multiply a rectangle's length and width to determine its area. Again, rather than telling your child the formula, the teacher guides him or her in determining the formula on his or her own.

Doing additional examples reflective of the one above reinforces your child's understanding of area of a rectangle and its related formula. Watch that he or she counts his or her squares in a way that squares aren't repeated. Emphasize counting all the squares across each row before starting to count squares down the sides, or in other rows.

Fourth Grade Scene

This example is about area and perimeter.

Example: You have 20 units of fencing to create a square or rectangular enclosed space for animals on a farm. How many ways can you create such a space? What do you notice about the areas of the spaces you create?

Classroom Action Steps:

- Children are given graph paper to create the spaces for the animals and record the dimensions, perimeter, and area. Since each space must use 20 units of fencing, all the spaces will have the same *perimeter*, or distance, around.

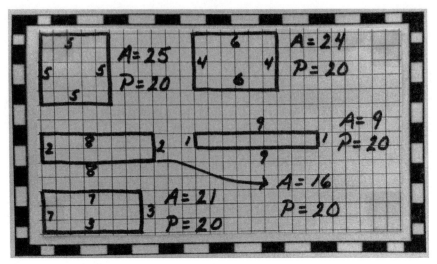

Figure 4.11 (Grade 4—Measurement and Data). *Source*: Regina M. Mistretta

- Children make rectangles of different lengths and widths, every time using all 20 units.
- Children are asked about the perimeters and areas of the enclosed spaces. The goal here is to have them discover how the areas differ while the perimeter remains constant at 20.

Parents Can:
Your child might think that he or she will use 20 squares to build the outside of the enclosed spaces. This is not the case because two sides of one square are counted at each corner. Doing additional examples reflective of the one above reinforces his or her understanding of relationships between perimeter and area.

In the above example, it was determined that areas among rectangles can differ, while the perimeter remains constant. Explore with your child whether or not perimeters among rectangles can differ, while the area remains constant. These are the types of explorations that develop your child's mind-set as a mathematical thinker and problem-solver.

Fifth Grade Scene

This is an example about the volume of a rectangular three-dimensional space.

Example: Regina needs to buy a doghouse for her pet, Jacob. She sees a nice one at the store. It is 5 units long by 3 units wide by 4 units high. What is the

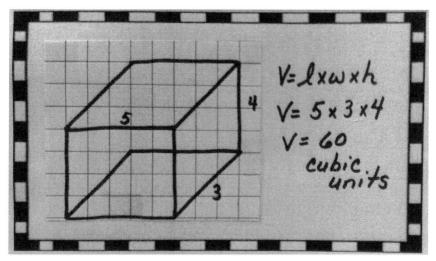

Figure 4.12 (Grade 5—Measurement and Data). *Source*: Regina M. Mistretta

volume of the space inside the doghouse? Write a formula for finding volume of a rectangular solid that could be used for any length, width, and height.

Classroom Action Steps:

- Explain to children that *volume* is a three-dimensional measure about how much space an object takes up. Since volume is measured in cubic units, they are given snap cubes to model the volume of the doghouse described in the above example. The scene above illustrates these snap cubes on grid paper.
- Using the snap cubes, children build a 5 by 3 rectangle to represent the bottom layer of space inside the doghouse.
- Children are asked:
  ○ How many cubic units are in this layer of the doghouse?
  In forming a response, children are guided to count the cubes, and multiply 5 × 3 to find the answer.
- Next, children are instructed to continue building upon this bottom layer of cubes until their model is 4 units high. This model represents the space inside the doghouse.
- Children are then asked:
  ○ How many cubic units are in the model?
  The goal here is to guide children to determine the answer to the question above by multiplying the number of cubic units in each layer by the number of layers (15 × 4).

- Children record their answer and are instructed to look for a way to arrive at that answer without using the cubes. It is here where children are positioned to determine the formula for the volume of a rectangular three-dimensional space.
  The formula for volume that children are guided to determine is as follows: Volume = (length) × (width) × (height).

Parents Can:

The formula for volume of a rectangular three-dimensional space is constructed by your child, rather than given to him or her by the teacher. As previously explained, this approach is conducive to deeper understanding and serves to cultivate a problem-solving mind-set for making sense of math.

Doing additional examples reflective of the one above reinforces your child's understanding of volume. He or she may struggle with seeing the connection between multiplying the three dimensions together, and multiplying the bottom layer by the solid's height. If so, inform him or her that multiplying length by width is the same as calculating the area of the bottom layer, or *base*. In turn, this amount of space is multiplied by the solid's height to calculate the entire amount of space inside the three-dimensional space.

Geometry

Third Grade Scene

This is an example about partitioning shapes into equal areas.

Example: With pattern blocks, divide a rhombus into equal triangles. How many triangles did you use? What fraction of the rhombus does one triangle represent?

Classroom Action Steps:

- Children use pattern blocks to see how many triangles can be put together to form a rhombus.
- Children are told that since they are making a rhombus with smaller equal pieces (triangles), each piece is a fraction of the whole rhombus. Children are then asked:
  ○ How many triangles are needed to make a rhombus?
  ○ What fraction of the rhombus does one triangle represent?
- Explained to children is that the total number of smaller parts is the *denominator* of the fraction and that since they are looking for a fraction name for

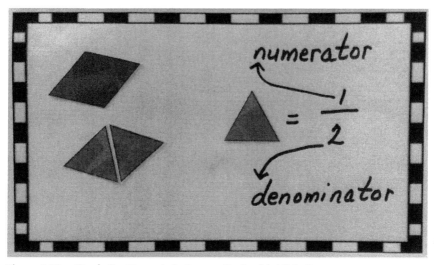

Figure 4.13 (Grade 3—Geometry). *Source:* Regina M. Mistretta

1 triangle, the *numerator* of the fraction is 1. The fraction ½, or one out of the two triangles, is then written to accompany the model and represent the triangle as one half of the rhombus.

Parents Can:
Doing additional examples reflective of the one above supports your child's understanding of fractions and of how to partition a whole into equal-sized pieces. For example, try partitioning a trapezoid into triangles; this will support your child's understanding of a triangle as 1/3 of a trapezoid. The triangle takes on different fraction names because its fraction name is dependent on the pattern block that serves as the whole.

Your child may try to make the whole with different-sized pattern blocks. If so, explain to him or her that the smaller shapes creating the whole must all be of the same size.

Printable pattern blocks can be accessed at http://mason.gmu.edu/%Emankus/Handson/manipulatives.htm.

Fourth Grade Scene

This is an example about symmetry.

Example: Below is half of a design that a *fourth grader* made with pattern blocks for the school art show. The other half has gone missing! Complete the design so that the design can be displayed at the school art show.

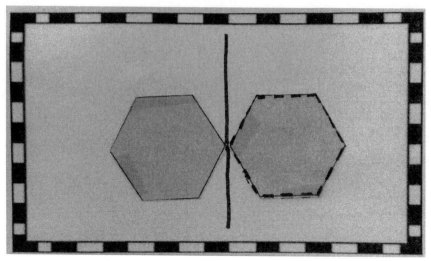

Figure 4.14   (Grade 4—Geometry). *Source:* Regina M. Mistretta

Classroom Action Steps:

- Explain to children that this task involves *symmetry*, meaning a balance of size, form, and arrangement. They are given pattern blocks and a ruler to create a mirror image.
- Using a ruler, a vertical line is drawn to help create the mirror image from top to bottom. Piece by piece, children trace the pattern blocks on one side of the line and create a duplicate image on the other side of the line.
- Children are instructed to check that their work is symmetrical by placing the pattern blocks onto the tracings, as well as by folding the paper along the vertical line to check that the parts completely overlap each other.

Parents Can:
Creating additional symmetrical designs with your child reinforces his or her understanding of symmetry. He or she may try to complete the design by repeating shapes only on one side of the design. If so, emphasize the need to reflect the shapes on both sides.

The action of folding the paper along the vertical line, known as the *line of symmetry*, can also support your child's understanding of the requirements involved when working with this math idea of symmetry.

Printable pattern blocks can be accessed at http://mason.gmu.edu/%Emankus/Handson/manipulatives.htm.

Fifth Grade Scene

This is an example about locating points on a coordinate plane.

Example: Find the ordered pair (3,2) on a grid.

Classroom Action Steps:

- Children are given grid paper and a marker.
- Explained to children is that an *ordered pair* tells how to locate a point on a grid. Two numbers are involved; the first one tells how far to the right the point is, and the second tells how far up. In addition, children are told that an ordered pair always describes a location where two lines intersect, or meet.
- Next, children are guided to find the ordered pair (3,2) on the grid.

Parents Can:

Discussing ordered pairs at home with your child reinforces his or her understanding of coordinates and how to locate them on a coordinate plane. You can do this as a game! You and your child can each use a grid and place three markers at specific points. Label your points on the grid. Put some sort of barrier between you and your child and try guessing where each other's markers are located. The first to find all three markers is the winner!

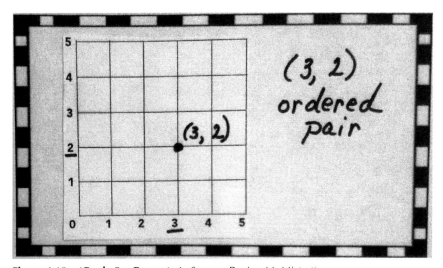

Figure 4.15 (Grade 5—Geometry). *Source:* Regina M. Mistretta

Your child may have difficulty remembering which coordinate indicates the vertical location and which indicates the horizontal location. To help him or her, relate finding coordinates to running and jumping. When runners compete, sometimes they jump over hurdles. First, they run, and then they jump. The same idea holds for locating coordinates on a grid. First, you move forward, and then up.

Chapter 5

Big Math Ideas in Grades 6–8

This chapter joins chapters 3 and 4 in providing descriptions about how big math ideas develop across the grades; this chapter focuses on Grades 6 through 8. A sampling of grade-level examples, entitled *Classroom Scenes*, provides an insider's view into how content unfolds in these grade-level classrooms. Coupled with these scenes are guidelines for parents about how to support such learning at home.

DEVELOPING CONTENT

Ratios and Proportional Relationships

The concepts of ratios and proportional relationships are big ideas that permeate Grades 6 and 7. Before discussing specific grade-level content, some related terms are defined at this point. A *ratio* is a comparison of two quantities such as the number of boys in a classroom as compared to the number of girls in that same classroom. Ratio comparisons can be part-to-part, such as the number of boys to the number of girls, or part-to-whole, such as the number of boys in a class to the number of students in that class.

Rate is defined as a ratio that compares quantities of different measures, such as $100 for 5 admission tickets to the zoo. A *unit rate* refers to a part-to-one ratio. For example, if 5 admission tickets to the zoo cost $100, then 1 admission ticket costs $20 (a unit rate of 20 to 1).

A *proportion* is a statement indicating that two ratios are equivalent. Blueprint drawings and the actual structures they depict look alike because they are proportionate to one another. For example, a scale of 1/3 inch on a drawing to 1 foot of actual length is expressed as 1/3 = 1.

Proportional relationships help find missing information while problem-solving. For example, if the ratio of half-day to full-day admission tickets to the zoo purchased on any day is usually 4:5, and 12 half-day tickets were purchased one day, a proportion can be set up and solved to find out how many full-day tickets were most likely purchased that day.

In *sixth grade*, children start discovering how life is filled with proportional relationships. In addition to those described above, real-life examples include calculating the cost of a food item when knowing the price per pound, determining a weekly pay rate given an hourly wage, and determining a distance represented on a map using the map's scale.

In *seventh grade*, children further develop their understanding of ratios by learning how to solve single- and multistep ratio and percent problems. *Seventh graders* graph proportional relationships and learn about how the unit rate is a measure of the steepness of a related line, called the *slope*. In addition, the percent problems solved in *seventh grade* include simple interest, taxes, tips, commissions, markups, discounts, and percent increases and decreases.

The Number System

As described in previous chapters, the base ten number system, or "place value" system, determines the value of numerals based on their position. For example, 6 in 16 has a value of 6 ones or 6, whereas 6 in 61 has a value of 6 tens or 60. *Sixth graders* continue developing their overall understanding of numbers by representing numbers in different ways based on the existing relationships among them. They extend their number understanding to include negative numbers along with whole numbers, fractions, and decimals.

In *seventh grade*, children further explore *rational numbers*: integers, fractions, decimals, and percent. These rational numbers can be written as fractions and as decimals that repeat (e.g., $4/3 = 1.33333...$) or terminate (e.g., $5/4 = 1.25$). *Seventh graders* apply and extend previously learned ideas concerning addition, subtraction, multiplication, and division to any of the rational numbers. For example, they may find the sum of $-11 + 6$ by locating -11 on a number line, moving 6 spaces in the positive direction, and understanding that the number they land on (-5) is the sum.

In addition, children apply previously learned long-division skills to learn about the difference between terminating and repeating decimals. *Seventh graders* build on their previous work with order of operations to solve problems with rational numbers. This expanded view supports their work with algebraic expressions as they rewrite expressions in different forms in order to solve problems. They also experience negative numbers in everyday contexts to build their confidence when using them.

Eighth graders explore *irrational numbers*, meaning numbers that cannot be expressed as ratios. When one converts irrational numbers to decimals, these numbers have endless, nonrepeating digits to the right of the decimal point. Examples of irrational numbers are $\pi \approx 3.14592$ and $\sqrt{2} \approx 1.4114213$. The approximation sign ($\approx$) is used here because these numbers never end and are therefore expressed in rounded form.

In-depth discussion is facilitated in *eighth grade* about why the differences between rational and irrational numbers matter. It is explained to the *eighth graders* that using numbers arose from the practical need to count objects. In ancient times, people counted objects as units, such as 1, 2, 3 "oranges."

Over time, the need for additional numbers grew as the need to measure developed. A need to express numbers between 0 and 1, 1 and 2, 2 and 3, and so on surfaced. Precise measuring had to account for all places on a ruler, and rational and irrational numbers allowed for that type of precision. Hence, all rational and irrational numbers can be found or approximated on a number line, and, in turn, they make counting possible to its fullest extent.

Expressions and Equations

Children in *sixth grade* build upon their algebraic thinking and reasoning skills learned in previous grades, particularly their work with discerning relationships and patterns. *Algebra* is a "language" for expressing real-world situations with math phrases or statements.

An algebraic *expression* is a combination of numbers, *variables* (unknown quantities represented with letters), and *operations* (addition, subtraction, multiplication, division) performed on them. Examples of expressions include $a + b$ and $3x - 5$. An algebraic *equation* is a statement that indicates equality between expressions, such as $3x - 5 = 2x + 3$. Now, while an equation states that two expressions are equal, an *inequality* may state that one expression is less than another.

Sixth graders start learning how to work with expressions and equations. Their discernment of relationships and patterns helps them expect outcomes and predict solutions, which they monitor and adjust accordingly. This process supports them in becoming mathematically proficient.

Seventh graders work with linear expressions involving rational coefficients. *Linear expressions* are those expressions where variables are not raised to a power other than 1. An example of a linear expression is $4x + 6$, where 4 is a *coefficient*, or the number in front of the variable x. 4x indicates that the expression is linear, as opposed to $4x^2$ where the variable x is raised to the power of 2, as opposed to the understood power of 1 in the original expression 4x.

Seventh graders use equivalent expressions to solve problems. They learn that changing the form of expressions to related quantities can support their solving of problems by making computations more manageable. In addition, they assess the reasonableness of answers by using mental computation and estimation strategies.

In *eighth grade*, children continue developing their versatility with expressions. They focus on expressing numbers using exponents and work with square roots and cube roots. *Roots* are the answers to examples involving exponents of 2 (square roots) and 3 (cube roots).

Eighth graders further develop understanding of unit rates and proportions, as well as deepen their understanding about linear equations. *Linear equations* represent straight lines, and *eighth graders* develop understanding about the slope of such lines.

Functions

In *eighth grade*, the idea of *function* is introduced. A function is a correspondence that associates each given input with exactly one output. For example, if the function is x + 3, then for every numerical value of x (*input*) there will be exactly one numerical outcome (*output*). For example, if x is 0, the outcome is 3 (0 + 3); if x is 1, the outcome is 4 (1 + 3); if x is 2, the outcome is 5 (2 + 3); and so on.

Functions are the focus for much of the algebra learned in high school and college. Therefore, children at this level are readied for such high-level math through hands-on activities involving straight lines that represent real-life contexts for study of functions.

Geometry

Sixth grade focuses on reasoning about area, surface area, and volume. Children further develop skills using visual tools for representing shapes such as through graphing and use of *nets* (flat outlines of three-dimensional shapes).

As previously defined, *area* is the amount of surface covered in an enclosed space. *Sixth graders* continue learning about the use of square units to calculate area and to find the areas of triangles, quadrilaterals (shapes with four sides), and other straight-sided shapes.

While the term *area* is associated with two-dimensional shapes, *surface area* refers to the area of the surface of three-dimensional objects, or solids. *Sixth graders* use nets to support them in finding surface areas of *prisms* and *pyramids*. A main difference between these two solids is that a prism has the same shape on the top and bottom of it, while a pyramid's sides come together at a common point.

Volume is the space filled, or occupied, by a three-dimensional object. Volume is measured in cubic units, and *sixth graders* physically and mentally use cubic units to build objects that they investigate. These hands-on geometry experiences support their understanding of the formulas they use while solving problems involving these geometric ideas.

Seventh graders reason about relationships among two-dimensional shapes using scale drawings and informal geometric constructions. They learn about relationships between angles formed by intersecting lines, as well as about characteristics of angles that form triangles.

Seventh graders work with three-dimensional shapes by relating them to two-dimensional shapes through examination of cross-sections. They solve problems involving area and circumference of a circle. *Area of a circle* refers to the amount of space enclosed by the circle, while *circumference* refers to the distance around the circle, or its perimeter.

Seventh graders solve problems involving area, volume, and surface area of two- and three-dimensional objects. As previously explained, *surface area* is the total area that can be measured on an entire three-dimensional surface. Think of it as finding the amount of wrapping paper you need to cover a package. *Volume*, on the other hand, refers to how much space is filled, or occupied. Think of this as the amount a carton can hold.

Eighth graders explore angles and use ideas about similarity and congruence to describe and analyze two-dimensional shapes. Shapes that are *congruent* have the same shape and size. Shapes are *similar* when their corresponding angles are equal, and their corresponding sides are in proportion. In other words, similar shapes are the same shape, but not necessarily the same size. *Eighth graders* will *rotate* (turn), *reflect* (flip), *translate* (slide), and *dilate* (resize) to determine whether or not two shapes are similar.

Eighth graders also learn about the *Pythagorean theorem*, which states that for any *right triangle* (a triangle containing a 90-degree angle) the sum of the squares of its *legs* (sides) equals the square of its hypotenuse. The *hypotenuse* is the side opposite the right angle (90-degree angle).

For example, a right triangle with legs of 3 and 4 feet has a hypotenuse of 5 feet because $3^2 + 4^2 = 5^2$, or $9 + 16 = 25$. Knowledge about this relationship between the sides of a right triangle helps *eighth graders* in solving problems involving practical situations such as constructions that involve determining the amount of materials needed to build a clubhouse with right triangles at its base.

Statistics and Probability

When we discuss the "average" price per gallon of gasoline or the "chance" of rainfall, we are thinking about ideas associated with statistics and probability.

Statistics is the study of how to collect, summarize, and present data. *Probability* is the study of chance. The study of statistics and probability provides children with opportunities to reason about real-world questions, to construct arguments, and to critique the reasoning of others.

Probability is expressed mathematically as a number between 0 and 1 (e.g., a chance of snowfall of 8/10, or 0.8, or 80%). A probability near 0 means an event is unlikely, a probability of ½ means the event is neither likely nor unlikely, and a probability near 1 means an event is likely to occur. A probability of 0 means the event is impossible, while a probability of 1 means the event will definitely happen.

The focus in *sixth grade* is on learning about how to describe a distribution in terms of its center and spread. For example, if data involving the sums of two rolled die (2, 3, 4, 5, 6, 7, 8, 9, 10, 11, 12) is described, the *center* of distribution is 7 (middle sum), and the spread, known as the *range*, is 10 (12 − 2).

Students graph the results of experiments, such as this dice example, to see how the shape of the distribution provides a picture of these features (center and range), as well as supports predictions about future rolls of the dice.

Seventh graders develop their previous work with single-data distributions and address differences between two sets of data. Children are guided to recognize that it is challenging to gather data on an entire population (*data set*) and that a *random sample* can represent a total population and generate valid results.

In addition, *seventh graders* develop probability models and use them to determine probabilities of future events such as outcomes for tossing a coin, spinning, and winning at Lotto. They find probabilities of *compound events* as well, which consist of two or more *simple events*. For example, rolling one die is a simple event, while rolling two dice is a compound event.

Eighth grade children work with *bivariate data*, which mathematically means two-variable data, for example people's height and foot lengths. Data is usually represented graphically with a *scatter plot* that helps them recognize whether or not a relationship exists between variables. *Eighth graders* come to know that straight lines are used to model such data, and they use lines and data tables to solve related problems.

CLASSROOM SCENES

The classroom scenes shared in this section are adapted from those included in the book *Hands-On Standards* (published by ETA hand2mind), and they represent a sampling of what learning looks like in today's Grades 6 through 8 math classrooms. Examples are presented, classroom action steps outlined, and ways parents can provide related support at home described.

You can access paper materials and student pages reflective of those shared at http://www.hand2mind.com/hosstudent.

Ratios and Proportional Relationships

Sixth Grade Scene

This example is about using a proportion to determine an unknown quantity.

Example: Christina is painting the floor of a garage with a textured paint that wears well in all types of weather. She remembers that on a previous paint job it took 4 pints of paint to cover an area of 60 square feet. What was the ratio of pints to square feet for that job? How many pints will she need for this garage floor, which has an area of 90 square feet?

Classroom Action Steps:

- Children are given grid paper to represent a "garage floor" surface with 60 square feet. Please note that each side of a square on the grid paper represents one foot. In turn, each square represents one square foot.
- Children are asked:
  - How many pints of paint are needed to cover 60 square feet? Write this as a ratio.
  - Based on this ratio, how many square feet will 1 pint of paint cover?

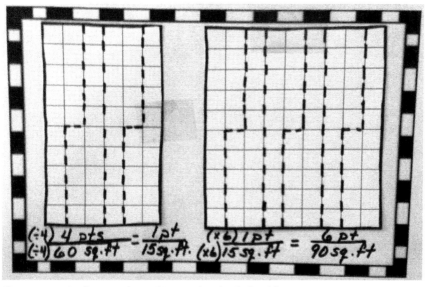

Figure 5.1 (Grade 6—Ratios and Proportional Relationships). *Source*: Regina M. Mistretta

- Children are then guided to divide the squares into 4 equal groups and express the answer as a ratio of 4/60 = 1/15.
- Next children are asked:
  - What is the area, in square feet, of the garage floor being painted?
- Children are guided to make a "garage floor" with 90 squares.
- Children are asked:
  - If 1 pint of paint covers 15 square feet, how many pints will Christina need to cover 90 square feet?
- Children are guided to write a proportion that represents this information and solve.

Parents Can:
You can reinforce this example at home with other amounts of squares. Because the concepts of *ratio* and *proportion* are closely related, your child may confuse them. You can support him or her in deeply understanding the meaning of the two terms by speaking with your child about the units involved and the relationships between these units.

Seventh Grade Scene

This is an example about proportional relationships and the constant of proportionality.

Example: Regina took her dog for a walk. In 6 minutes, she had walked 3 blocks. In 11 minutes, she had walked 6 blocks. If the number of blocks is proportional to the number of minutes, what is the constant of proportionality for the relationship?

Classroom Action Steps:

- Children are given a coordinate grid and asked to graph the relationship described in the example. Using the x-axis for time (minutes) and the y-axis for distance (blocks), children plot the points (6,3) to represent 6 minutes for 3 blocks walked and (12,6) to represent 12 minutes for 6 blocks walked. They then connect the points with a straight line extended through the *origin*, point (0,0).
- Discussed with children is that the relationship of minutes to blocks is proportional because 3/6 is equivalent to 6/12; in other words, both ratios can be simplified to 1/2. This can also be discussed with the ratios 6/3 = 12/6 = 2/1.
- Next, children are asked to determine how far up and across the graphed line one needs to travel in order to go from the point (6,3) to the point

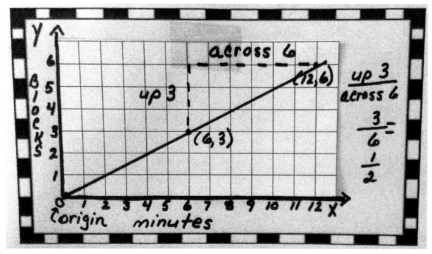

Figure 5.2 **(Grade 7—Ratios and Proprotional Relationships).** *Source:* Regina M. Mistretta

(12,6). The response elicited from children is that one travels up 3 units and across 6 units to go from one point to the other. In turn, 3/6 or 1/2 is labeled as the *constant of proportionality* because it tells how much the *y-coordinate* (value on the vertical axis) changes for each unit of change in the *x-coordinate* (value on the x-axis).
• Children are guided to select different points on the line to travel from and to as means for confirming the constant of proportionality as 1/2.

Parents Can:
Your child may have difficulty finding the vertical and horizontal distances between the points. If so, point out to him or her that drawing lines to represent the distances forms a right triangle with the line as shown in the above scene.

The Number System

Sixth Grade Scene

This example is about representing and ordering integers.

Example: Nicholas, Christina, and Jacob are playing a game. After one round of play, Nicholas lost 5 points, Christina gained 4 points, and Jacob lost 2 points. Use integers to represent the scores for this round of play. Which scores represent first and last place?

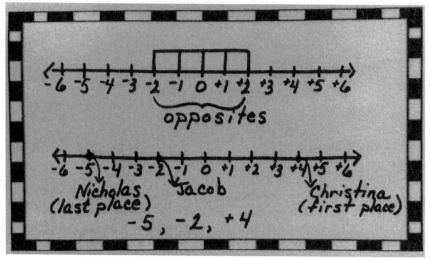

Figure 5.3 (Grade 6—The Number System). *Source*: Regina M. Mistretta

Classroom Action Steps:

- Children are given number lines and asked to show 2 squares to the left of 0 and 2 squares to the right of 0.
- It is explained to children that integers are the counting numbers, their opposites, and 0. Numbers −2 and 2 are explained as being opposites because they are the same distance from 0 on the number line.
- Children are given examples of what negative integers can represent, such as losses, below-zero temperatures, and below-sea-level altitudes. Likewise, examples of what positive integers can represent are shared with children such as the amount of points scored at a game, deposits to bank accounts, and above-zero temperatures.
- Children are then asked to represent the losses and gains described in the above example on another number line.
- Then children are told that number lines are used to compare and order integers and that the values of the numbers increase as one moves left to right. They are guided to use symbols to compare the three integers from the game described above, and write the integers in order from least to greatest.

Parents Can:
Your child may be confused by an integer such as −7 being less than −1. If so, use real-world contexts to help him or her see that the farther a negative integer is from 0, the less its value. For example, a person owing someone $7 has less money than a person owing someone $1.

Seventh Grade Scene

This is an example about adding integers.

Example: A football team lost 6 yards on one play and then gained 13 yards on the next play. What was the team's final gained yardage after the two plays?

Classroom Action Steps:

- Children are asked to represent this example on a number line. Children are guided to start at 0 and draw a segment that is 6 units to the left to represent the loss of yardage.
- From that point on the number line (–6), children draw a segment that is 13 units to the right to represent the gain in yardage.
- It is explained to children that the point where the second line segment ends (7) is the answer.

Parents Can:
Your child may confuse negative signs with minus signs. If so, have your child write the example –6 + 13 = 7. Explain to him or her that this equation is read as *negative six (not minus six) plus thirteen equals seven*. On a number line, show your child that –6 and 6 are opposites because both are 6 units from 0, only in opposite directions.

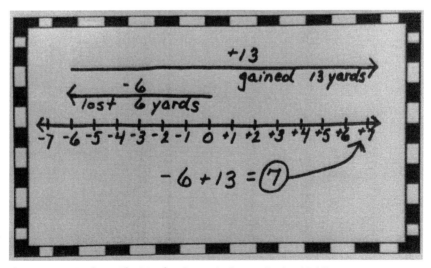

Figure 5.4 (Grade 7—The Number System). *Source*: Regina M. Mistretta

Eighth Grade Scene

This example is about estimating square roots.

Example: A principal of a school received a donation of linoleum tiles to cover a play area of 65 square feet of a preschool floor. The sides of the tiles each measure 1 foot. Describe the amount of tiles that can create the largest possible square play area.

Classroom Action Steps:

- Children use grid paper to model the example where each square represents a tile with sides measuring 1 foot. Children build up the following squares: $1 \times 1, 2 \times 2, 3 \times 3, 4 \times 4, 5 \times 5, 6 \times 6, 7 \times 7, 8 \times 8$, and 9×9. Then the area of each of these squares is calculated.
  Children understand from previous work that *square root* means a number that when multiplied by itself yields a number that can be represented as a square. For example, the square root of 4 is 2 because $2 \times 2 = 4$, a number of objects that can be arranged to form a square.
  It is explained to children that square roots are estimated to find the closest whole number (of squares, in this case) that can form a square as close to a given area (65 square feet, in this case).
- Children are then guided in determining which of the modeled play areas falls between the 65 square feet of the preschool floor. Children are asked:
  ○ Between which squares modeled does the area of 65 square feet fall?

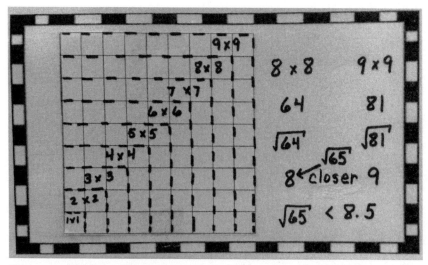

Figure 5.5   (Grade 8—The Number System). *Source*: Regina M. Mistretta

The response elicited from children is that 65 falls between the 8×8 square (the square representing 64 square feet) and the 9×9 square (the square representing 81 square feet).

○ Do you think the square root is greater or less than 8.5? Explain.

The response elicited from children is that the square root is less than 8.5 because 65 is closer to 64 than it is to 81.

• Children are then guided to conclude that the largest possible square play area that can be created is 64 square feet, modeled by 64 squares arranged as an 8 by 8 square.

Parents Can:

You can reinforce this example at home by doing similar examples with grid paper. Practice helps improve your child's skill with approximating square roots. He or she may need support in articulating how to estimate square roots by hearing you explain it first. Point out to him or her that the word *root* in math means "the answer" and that for a given number of squares, the square root of that number will yield the dimensions of the square he or she models.

Expressions and Equations

Sixth Grade Scene

This example is about expressions with a variable.

Example: It takes 5 minutes for Regina to get her station wagon washed. The total time needed to get station wagons washed depends upon arrival time.

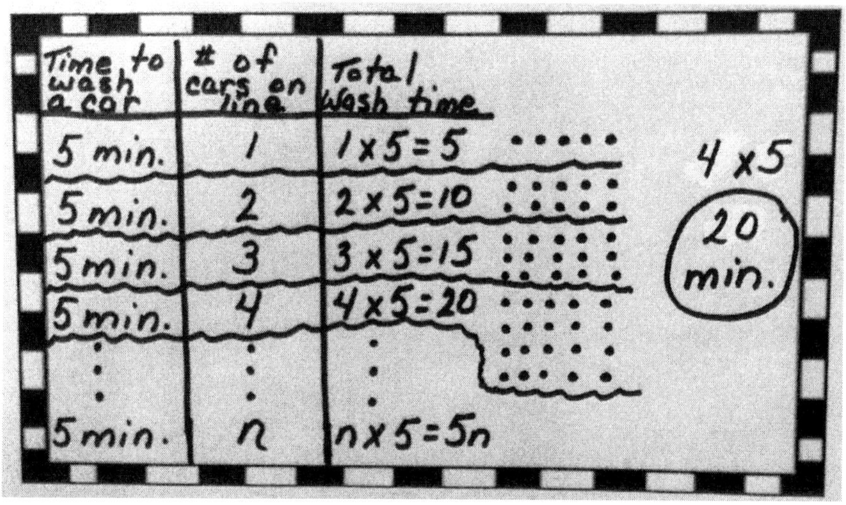

Figure 5.6 (Grade 6—Expressions and Equations). *Source:* Regina M. Mistretta

Write an expression to show how long it will take Regina to get her station wagon washed. Then evaluate the expression to determine how long it takes Regina to get her station wagon washed if she is 7th in line.

Classroom Action Steps:

- Children use dots to make an array to show how many minutes it will take Regina to get her station wagon washed if she is first in line.
- Children repeat this process for 2nd, 3rd, and 4th place in line and record findings in an organized table.
- Children are asked:
  ○ What changes in each situation?
     The term *variable* is introduced to children as the amount that varies; in this example, it is the position of the station wagon in line that varies, while the amount of time to wash the station wagon remains constant (5 minutes).
- Children are then asked to find the length of time for Regina to get her station wagon washed if she is 7th in line (n = 7), where n represents the place in line. Children are also informed that finding the value of an expression is called *evaluating*.

Parents Can:
Doing more of this type of example with your child reflects the type of engagement that reinforces your child's understanding of evaluating expressions. If your child is having difficulty writing variable expressions, ask him or her to first think about how numbers could change while something else remains constant to help him or her identify existing relationships for real-life situations. Once your child understands a relationship, he or she can then replace the varying or changing number with a letter.

Seventh Grade Scene

This example is about writing equations.

Example: Mia has $4 more than 5 times the amount of money that Bella has. Together they have 7 times the amount that Bella has. How much money do Mia and Bella each have?

Classroom Action Steps:

- Children are guided to express the amount of money each child has, as well as express the amount both children have together.
- Children then solve the equations by drawing them with the use of x marks.

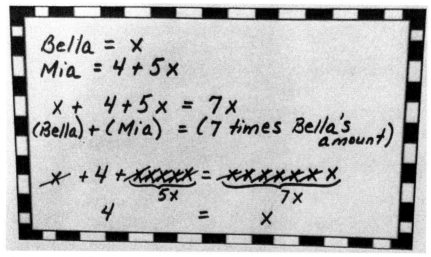

Figure 5.7 (Grade 7—Expressions and Equations). *Source:* Regina M. Mistretta

- Through pairing of the x marks, children conclude that x = 4. Pairing is represented in the above scene as cross-offs of two at a time.
- Using x = 4, children go on to determine that while Bella has $4, Mia has $24 (4 + 5(4)).

Parents Can:
Children sometimes stop working once they find the value of x. However, in this example, one needs to find the amount of money that each child has, not just Mia. If this applies to your child, ask him or her whether or not each child has $4. Explain to your child that he or she needs to take the x-value and apply it to the word problem in order to find the amount of money each child has. Bella has $4, while Mia has 4 + 5($4) or $24. In other words, make sure your child rereads the example to reinforce the original question.

Eighth Grade Scene

This is an example about squares and square roots.

Example: Use 55 square tiles to make 5 designs. Each design is a square and all squares are different sizes. How many tiles are used in each square design? What is the length of the sides in each square design?

Classroom Action Steps:

- Children are given grid paper to represent square tile designs with squares, and they record data about the squares and related square roots.

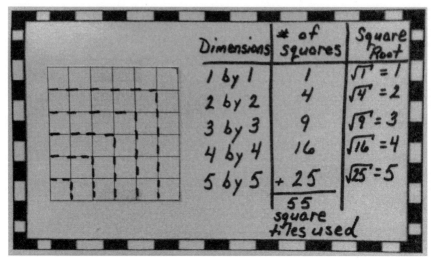

Figure 5.8   (Grade 8—Expressions and Equations). *Source:* Regina M. Mistretta

For a given number of tiles, the *square root* of that number gives the dimensions of the *square* that can be built with the tiles.

- On the grid paper, children are asked to build a 1 × 1 and a 2 × 2 square and find the number of tiles in each square. Children then write each square number.
- The *radical sign* is explained to children as meaning "find the square root." Children are then asked to indicate the part of the square that represents the *square root*, in order to guide their understanding of the side length of the square as representing the square root.
- Children build other squares and record corresponding data.

Parents Can:

If your child has difficulty finding the 5 smallest perfect squares, suggest that he or she start with one tile, add one tile to the row, and then add a tile to each column to make a square. *Perfect square* means an amount of tiles that can all be joined together to form a complete square.

Functions

Eighth Grade Scene

This is an example about graphing linear equations.

Example: While in an amusement park, two people are finding their way to a roller coaster. There are two paths they could follow. One path can be

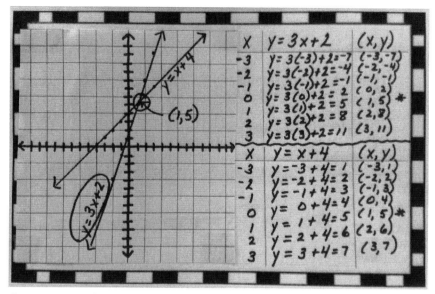

Figure 5.9 (Grade 8—Functions). *Source*: Regina M. Mistretta

mapped on a four-quadrant grid using the equation y = 3x + 2. The other path can be mapped using the equation y = x + 4. If the roller coaster is located at the origin, which path will take them closer to the roller coaster?

Classroom Action Steps:

- Children are given a recording chart and coordinate graphing paper. *Origin* is defined as the place on the coordinate graph where the x and y axes cross, (0,0).
- Children are asked to write the equation y = 3x + 2 and to calculate y values for the x values of −3, −2, −1, 0, 1, 2, and 3. They then write an ordered pair and plot the points. *Y values* are those along the vertical axis, while *x values* are those along the horizontal axis. *Ordered pair* means a point with both an x and y value.
- Children connect the ordered pairs and are guided to see how they form a straight line. Since the equation y = 3x + 2 forms a straight line, it is known as a *linear equation*.
- The previous two steps are repeated for the equation y = x + 4.
- Children are asked:
  ○ Does either graph pass through the origin?
  ○ Is there any point that is on both lines?
  The point that is on both lines represents the starting location of the two people in the amusement park. The line that comes closest to the origin

(y = 3x + 2) represents the path that will lead the pair closest to the roller coaster.

Parents Can:

This example represents a way to visually represent how algebra connects with real-life situations. If your child confuses the x- and y-coordinates, remind him or her that the ordered pair is arranged alphabetically, so the x-coordinate is written first.

Geometry

Sixth Grade Scene

This is an example about nets.

Example: Daniel works for a company that makes cardboard shipping containers. Each container is stored as a flat piece that can be assembled when needed. What might the flat cardboard piece look like for a cube container?

Classroom Action Steps:

• It is explained to children that a *net* is a pattern that can be folded to make a three-dimensional object. They are shown a three-dimensional solid, such as a cube, and its related net so as to point out the differences between a solid shape and its two-dimensional (flat) makeup.

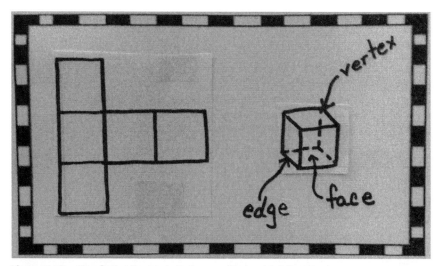

Figure 5.10 (Grade 6—Geometry). *Source*: Regina M. Mistretta

- Related vocabulary is discussed with children. Words include *faces*, or the flat surfaces, *edges*, or the straight sides, and *vertices*, or the corners.
- Children then cut out the net and use tape to construct a cube.

Parents Can:

Doing similar constructions with your child supports his or her understanding of three-dimensional shapes. The National Council of Teachers of Mathematics offers a virtual tool where you and your child can explore different solids and their corresponding faces, edges, and vertices. The link to this resource is http://www.nctm.org/Classroom-Resources/Interactives/Geometric-Solids/.

Seventh Grade Scene

This is an example about finding the circumference of a circle.

Example: Christina is exploring relationships that exist in circles. She measured the circumference and diameter of different-sized circles. She then divided the circumference measurements by the related diameter measurements. What did she notice?

Classroom Action Steps:

- Children are given circles of different sizes and a recording sheet to indicate measurements they gather about circles (circumference and diameter measured in centimeter units for this example).

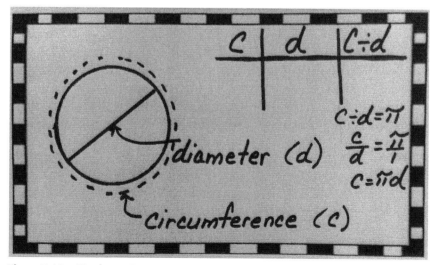

Figure 5.11 (Grade 7—Geometry). *Source*: Regina M. Mistretta

Circumference is the distance around a circle, while *diameter* is the difference from one side of a circle to the other side through the center of the circle. Measuring the diameter with a ruler is feasible; however, measuring circumference requires children to use string to measure around the circle first because the ruler cannot bend. Children then take that length of string and find its measure when placed onto the ruler.

- Children complete their chart and compute *quotients* (answers to division examples) by dividing each circle's circumference length by its corresponding diameter length.
- Children are asked about patterns they notice among the data recorded. The response elicited from children is that the quotients are all close to 3.14, which is the approximated value for the Greek letter pi (π). *Pi* was actually discovered by Greek mathematicians while measuring various-sized circular fountains.

It is an amazing math concept existing in our world that your children can discover and actually celebrate on National Pi Day which is March 14. This day was chosen as it is the third month of the year and fourteenth day of that month; 3.14. So when that day rolls around, have some pie. Before you eat it though, measure its circumference and diameter and compute π!

- Next, children are guided to determine a formula that can be used to determine the circumference of any circle when the diameter is known.
  - The relationship children previously discovered is written as $C \div d = \pi$, where C represents circumference and d represents diameter.
  - The equation is then rewritten in the equivalent form, $C/d = \pi/1$.
  - Children's previous work with solving proportions enables them to cross multiply and arrive at the formula $C = \pi d$.

Parents Can:

You can reinforce your child's understanding of circumference by measuring circles in your home and looking for patterns in your gathered data in ways reflective of the above scene. Make sure he or she measures each diameter and circumference correctly. Be sure he or she holds the string tautly while measuring circumference; and remind him or her to measure the diameter at the widest part of the circle. This will help your child calculate an accurate number for π.

In addition, reinforce with your child that π is the same for any circle, no matter how big or small. Calculations for π may differ slightly; however, all calculations will tend toward π. Recognizing this math relationship in the world is a great way for your child to appreciate math.

Even while baking cookies, discuss with your child the fact that as each of those cookies forms into a circular shape in the oven, a math relationship exists between each cookie's circumference and diameter.

Eighth Grade Scene

This is an example about reflections and lines of reflection.

Example: Mrs. Mistretta has a large vegetable garden shaped like a hexagon. She wants to be able to stand in the middle of the garden and look to one side, and then the other, and see the same shape, just as if she were looking in a mirror. What will Mrs. Mistretta's garden landscape plan look like?

Classroom Action Steps:

• Children are given coordinate graphing paper and asked to plot the points: (0,1), (1,0), (2,0), (3,1), (2,2), and (1,2). Children then connect the points to represent Mrs. Mistretta's hexagon-shaped vegetable garden.
• Children reflect the image of the hexagon over the y-axis, known as the *line of reflection*, and record the coordinates of the new points in a table.
• Children compare the coordinates of the preimage (before the reflection) to the postimage (after the reflection) to support their determination that the x values are opposites of each other, while the y values remain the same. Please note that 0 is considered neither positive nor negative.

Parents Can:

By working through this example, your child determines what happens to the coordinates as a result of a reflection over the y-axis. Rather than being told what will happen, your child discovers it, a meaningful learning experience he or she will understand because of active engagement in it.

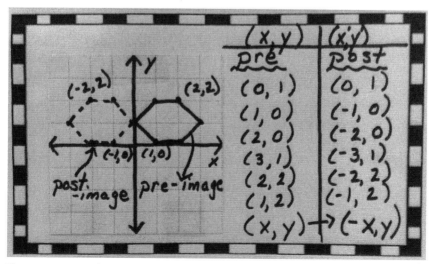

Figure 5.12 (Grade 8—Geometry). *Source*: Regina M. Mistretta

Students tend to forget the rules for reflections, as well as slides and turns, because they only memorize rules given to them. So please encourage your child to actively explore what happens mathematically. His or her developed understanding will be far deeper for it, and, in turn, he or she will retain such understanding.

Statistics and Probability

Sixth Grade Scene

This example is about describing distributions.

Example: Coach Mistretta collected data on his hockey team for two seasons. The table shows his data for shots on goal. Make a display of the data. Describe the distribution of values. Is the distribution symmetric? Explain.

Classroom Action Steps:

- Children are given a data table and dot paper to display the data.
  The numbers across represent the shots on goal, while the dots represent the corresponding number of games. For example, 1 dot above the 12 represents 1 game having 12 shots on goal.
- Children engage in conversation about the shape of the data plot. The response elicited from children is the fact that the data has *symmetry*, meaning that the data is equally distributed about a center value (or nearly so).

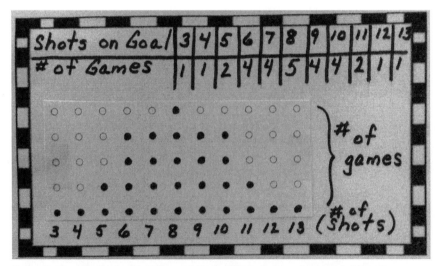

Figure 5.13   (Grade 6—Statistics and Probability). *Source:* Regina M. Mistretta

Also discussed is that 29 games are represented, the median is the 17th game, and the range is 10 (13 – 3). As previously defined in another sixth-grade classroom scene, *median* is the middle value and *range* is the span of values.

Parents Can:

The goal of this activity is to further develop your child's understanding of data and how to represent data. Doing additional examples reflective of the one above supports your child's skills with collecting, representing, and interpreting data. So, start collecting, representing, and talking about data!

Seventh Grade Scene

This example is about theoretical and experimental probability.

Example: What does it mean when one says the probability of rolling a 3 on a die is 1/6?

Classroom Action Steps:

• Explained to children is that *theoretical probability* of an event is determined with the formula involving the number of favorable outcomes divided by the number of possible outcomes. For example, the probability of rolling a 3 on a die is 1/6 because there is one 3 on a die among 6 possibilities.

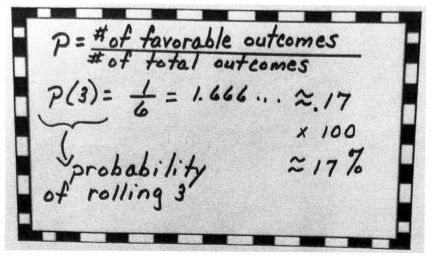

Figure 5.14 **(Grade 7—Statistics and Probability).** *Source:* Regina M. Mistretta

Experimental probability, on the other hand, is what actually happens. For example, when one actually rolls a die, it doesn't necessarily mean that after 6 rolls, one will have rolled exactly one 3.

- To develop understanding of the above explanation, children are given a die and asked to roll it 100 times, keeping track of the number of times a 3 is rolled.
- Data is gathered from each member in the class. This data is converted into percentages and analyzed for possible patterns.
- Children are guided to see how all the percentages tend to be 17%, which is 1/6 as a percentage rounded to the nearest whole number.
- It is explained to children that the more one would roll the die, the closer the percentage of 3s would come to be 17%.

Parents Can:

Rolling the die additional times, as described above, supports your child in seeing how the experimental probability answer comes closer and closer to the theoretical probability answer over time. Doing additional experiments with probabilities for rolling other numbers on a die helps reinforce your child's understanding of the meaning behind saying the probability of an event happening is 1/6 for any number on a die.

In addition, having conversations with your child about the probability ideas behind games of chance supports his or her decision-making process when determining the likelihood of events happening. Try rolling two dice and having conversation about the probabilities of the sums of those rolls.

Eighth Grade Scene

This is an example about scatter plots and correlations.

Example: The coach of the baseball team is reviewing some statistics for the first six games of the season. Is there a positive correlation, a negative correlation, or no correlation between hours of practice and the number of hits the team got, or between hours of practice and the number of errors the team made?

Classroom Action Steps:

- Children are given coordinate graphing paper to first plot the coordinate pairs for hours of practice (x) and number of hits (y).
- Children are asked to examine the graph. It is explained to them that when one variable gets larger as the other variable gets larger, the two variables

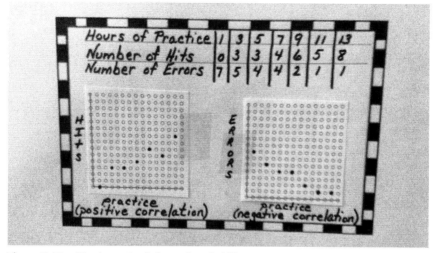

Hours of Practice	1	3	5	7	9	11	13
Number of Hits	0	3	3	4	6	5	8
Number of Errors	7	5	4	4	2	1	1

Figure 5.15   (Grade 8—Statistics and Probability). *Source:* Regina M. Mistretta

have a *positive correlation.* The graph will appear to go upward from the y-axis.

If one variable gets smaller as the other gets larger, the two variables have a *negative correlation,* and the graph will appear to go downward from the y-axis.

No correlation exists when one cannot determine to which direction the graph is moving because a relationship among the numbers does not exist.

- Children are asked:
  ○ Which way do the points go?
  ○ Does the data show a positive correlation, a negative correlation, or no correlation?
- Children repeat the previous two steps for hours of practice (x) and number of errors (y).

Parents Can:

If your child thinks that the coordinate pairs should form a perfect line, reassure him or her that the points do not need to do this in order to show a correlation. Point out to him or her that determining correlations about data often helps determine solutions for real-world situations. The point, again, is to support your child in developing his or her awareness of math in the world.

Chapter 6

Collaborative Anchor Tasks

This chapter offers *collaborative anchor tasks*, so termed for their ability to connect parents and children with math across the grades. The tasks serve as additional entry points for parents to engage in conversation with their child about math thinking. The tasks are framed in a manner so as to provide both (a) math content information and (b) guidelines for supporting children in making sense of math.

CONCEPT CARDS

Concept cards are teaching tools that support visualization of, and communication about, math concepts.

Examples and nonexamples of a concept are illustrated with various representations. Children eliminate irrelevant characteristics and identify essential ones in order to formulate definitions that contain necessary and sufficient information. The third part of the card guides children to distinguish between correct and incorrect examples, a task that strengthens analytical skills. Children are then prompted to share examples and nonexamples, along with a definition they develop. The cards at this point spark creative thinking and provide opportunities for discussion about different solutions and related justifications.

The goal is to guide children's understanding of perpendicular lines as those that cross and form 90-degree angles, or spaces into which one could exactly fit the corner of a piece of paper. One need not break out the protractor to determine whether or not an angle measures 90 degrees. It's as simple

These are pairs of perpendicular lines.

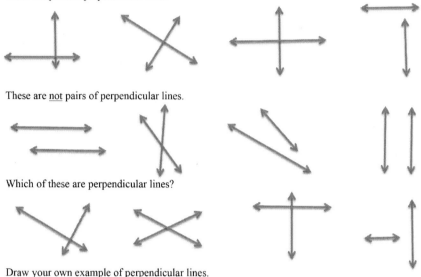

These are <u>not</u> pairs of perpendicular lines.

Which of these are perpendicular lines?

Draw your own example of perpendicular lines.

Draw your own non-example of perpendicular lines.

What are perpendicular lines?

Figure 6.1   (Concept Card). *Source*: Regina M. Mistretta

as using that corner of a piece of paper to represent such an amount of space between two lines. Call it a "right angle tester" and use it as a means for identifying real-life examples and nonexamples of right angles!

Take a closer look at the last example in the first row; the lines are purposely not crossing. This example is there to minimize a misunderstanding among children that lines need to physically cross on paper. The arrows at the ends of lines represent the fact that lines continue on forever (infinitely). So, in this example, the lines will eventually cross and form 90-degree angles. Other concept cards can be accessed at http://tinyurl.com/ltpw6af to print and discuss with children.

Parents Can:
- Pose questions to guide your child's thinking while analyzing the concept cards.
  - How are the examples in the first row alike?
  - How are the nonexamples in the second row different from the examples in the first row?
- Encourage your child to illustrate and form definitions. This allows your child to convey content material in a manner that actively involves him or her in using analysis and classification skills; these skills are necessary components of algebraic thinking.
- Talk with your child's teacher about specific grade-level math topics for which you and your child could use or create concept cards.

ATTRIBUTE PIECES

An attribute piece set can comprise 32 pieces consisting of four shapes (triangle, circle, square, and hexagon) in four colors (yellow, red, green, and blue) and two sizes (small and big). Printable attribute pieces can be found at http://tinyurl.com/ltpw6af.

Lineups

In this task, children arrange attribute pieces into a line where every piece differs from the one after it in one, two, or three ways. For example, in a 1-difference line, a big red square could follow a big, green square, with the one difference being color. For a 2-difference line, a small, yellow circle could follow a big, green circle, with the two differences being size and color. For a 3-difference line, a big, red hexagon could follow a small, blue circle, with the three differences being size, color, and shape.

Parents Can:
- Ask your child to explain how the attribute pieces he or she chooses for the lineups are the same and different from one another.
- Have your child investigate whether or not it is possible to have all of the small pieces at the beginning of a lineup. Reason with him or her about why or why not.
- The amount of pieces used and the lineup requirements will depend on your child's grade level. Discuss with your child's teacher the circumstances that would best support him or her.

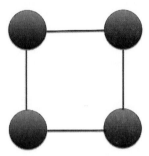

Figure 6.2   (Attribute Pieces Puzzle). *Source*: Regina M. Mistretta

Puzzles

Puzzles also provide opportunities for children to reason with attribute pieces. Children place attribute pieces into each of the circle areas. If the circles are connected with one line, the attribute pieces children choose to place into those circles must differ in one way (either by size, color, or shape). If the circles are connected with two lines, the attribute pieces need to differ in two ways. And if the circles are connected with three lines, the attribute pieces differ in three ways.

Other puzzles can be found at http://tinyurl.com/ltpw6af.

Parents Can:
• Ask your child to explain to you how the attribute pieces he or she chooses for the puzzles are the same and different from one another.
• The complexity of the puzzle depends on the grade level involved. Discuss with your child's teacher the circumstances that would best support him or her.

PATTERN BLOCK STRUCTURES

This task uses particular pattern blocks, namely yellow hexagons, red trapezoids, blue rhombii, and green triangles. With this task, children can engage in problem-solving around a computational question, and this hinges on children's understandings of the fractional relationships existing among the pieces. Printable pattern blocks can be found at http://mason.gmu.edu/%Emankus/Handson/manipulatives.htm.

The fractional relationships that exist among the blocks are as follows:

• Two red trapezoids cover a yellow hexagon; in other words, a red trapezoid is one-half of a yellow hexagon.

- Three rhombii cover a yellow hexagon; in other words, a rhombus is one-third of a yellow hexagon.
- Six green triangles cover a yellow hexagon; in other words, a green triangle is one-sixth of a yellow hexagon.

Children may choose to call them by their shape name, color name, or fraction name. Ultimately, they should use all the names for the pattern blocks as they develop understandings about fractions. Such understandings can later be used to solve a computational task with these blocks.

Please note that the fraction names for the blocks as discussed above are true when the yellow hexagon serves as the whole that is cut into equally sized portions. Other pieces can serve as the whole as well, as was described in a classroom scene in chapter 4.

Parents Can:
- Initiate free play with the pattern blocks to develop the understandings described above. Pose the following guiding questions to your child:
  ○ What pattern blocks can be joined together to form a yellow hexagon?
  ○ How many red trapezoids cover a yellow hexagon?
  ○ How many blue rhombii cover a yellow hexagon?
  ○ How many green triangles cover a yellow hexagon?
  ○ How many green triangles cover a blue rhombus?
  ○ How many green triangles cover a red trapezoid?
- Use the discoveries from the above free play and related questioning to discuss with your child how the red trapezoid is half of the yellow hexagon, the blue rhombus a third of the yellow hexagon, and the green triangle a sixth of the yellow hexagon.
- Revisit the first question with your child
  ○ *What pattern blocks can be joined together to form a yellow hexagon?*

You now have an opportunity to converse with your child about answers to that question using the pattern blocks' fraction names, as opposed to just their color or shape names.

For example, one whole yellow hexagon can be covered by one-half, one-third, and one-sixth. Such a conversation reflects addition of fractions with unlike denominators.

Discuss further with your child other solutions to the question, such as two greens and two blues (two-sixths plus two-thirds equaling one whole). This is a meaningful informal concrete experience that builds a strong foundation for understanding the rule for adding fractions with unlike denominators.

• This task can transition into a computational exercise. At this point, you and your child have discovered that two greens cover a blue, three greens cover a red, and six greens cover a yellow.

  Assign a monetary value to the green triangle. For once the green triangle is assigned a value; the value of the other pattern blocks can be calculated. For example, double (or add twice) the green's value to arrive at the value of the blue, triple (or add three times) the green's value to find the value of the red, and multiple the green's value by six (or add six times) to find the value of the yellow.

  You and your child may opt to find the monetary values using other strategies. For example, the hexagon's value can be arrived at by adding the value of the trapezoid to that of the rhombus and the triangle, another previously discovered relationship. This is wonderful! Encourage your child to determine solutions in multiple ways; it deepens their understanding about the math involved.

• Further the fun by designing structures with as many pattern blocks as your child wants to use. Once constructed, the task is to compute the structure's monetary value.
  ○ Pose the question: How much does your structure cost if a green triangle costs $1.89?
  ○ Allow exploration, questioning and multiple strategies, observe and guide—refrain from telling—and give hints if needed.
  ○ Pose the question: What adaptation could you make to the cost of the green triangle so that the total cost of your design would now increase by more than a dollar, but not more than two dollars? (Same recommendations as in the previous step.)

  The task as written is appropriate for Grades 3 through 5. Answers can be arrived at in multiple ways, and you should encourage your child to recalculate his or her answer using a different method than the one he or she originally used. Arriving at answers in multiple ways can deepen your child's understanding.

  If your child is younger, the task can be adapted so that the green triangle costs 1¢, 2¢, or 5¢ cents. Your child could then discuss how to make the cost of their design increase or decrease. If your child is older, then he or she can compute using larger numbers and discuss how to make the total cost increase by more than 10%, but not more than 15%.

MONSTER COMBOS

This task engages children in exploring combinations. By joining the different heads, bodies, and feet shown below to create a monster, children concretely develop understandings for the meaning of a combination. A *combination* is a way of selecting items from a collection where the order of selection does not matter.

These monster parts can be found at http://tinyurl.com/ltpw6af. An example of one of 12 possible monsters follows.

Parents Can:

- Create and pictorially represent with your child all 12 monsters.
- Ask your child to list all the combinations of monster parts.
- Ask your child how to determine the total number of possible combinations numerically.
- Guide him or her to see how they can arrive at the answer of 12 by multiplying the number of possible heads (2) by the number of possible bodies (3) by the number of possible feet (2). This number manipulation is known as the *counting principle* for determining the number of possible combinations.

This task as written is appropriate for Grades 3 and 4. If your child is younger, he or she can also engage in this activity by concretely building the

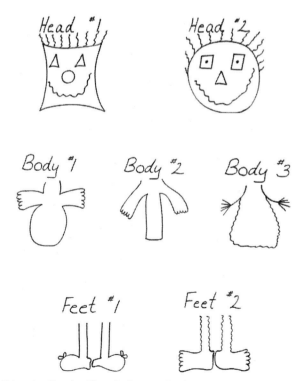

Figure 6.3 **(Monster Combo Pieces).** *Source:* Regina M. Mistretta

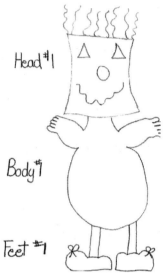

Figure 6.4   (Sample Monster). *Source*: Regina M. Mistretta

different monsters using fewer pieces. A related interactive tool for prekindergarten through Grade 5, entitled Bobbi Bear, can be found on the NCTM
website at http://illuminations.nctm.org/Activity.aspx?id=3540.

Monster combos can be adapted if your child is older as well. Consider
contexts such as creating sandwiches, coffee drinks, outfits, or license plates.
Provide the related choices for each context and list the possible combinations.

Whichever grade your child is in or context you are using, the objective is
for him or her to concretely discover the procedure for finding and representing the total number of possible combinations. Such a learning experience
reflects your child's math classroom; one where he or she constructs understandings about math ideas and procedures, rather than memorizes what is
merely told to him or her.

WEB-BASED RESOURCES

Across all grade levels, Khan Academy (www.khanacademy.org) supports
content knowledge. Mobile apps are available from the NCTM at http://
illuminations.nctm.org/content.aspx?id=3855. In addition, this organization's

website contains interactive online resources families can use according to the grade-level bands listed below.

Pre-K through Grade 2
• http://illuminations.nctm.org/Search.aspx?view=search&type=ac&gr= Pre-K-2

Grades 3 through 5
• http://illuminations.nctm.org/Search.aspx?view=search&type=ac&gr=3-5

Grades 6 through 8
• http://illuminations.nctm.org/Search.aspx?view=search&type=ac&gr=6-8

Grades 9 through 12
• http://illuminations.nctm.org/Search.aspx?view=search&type=ac&gr=9-12

Additional related family resources provided by the NCTM relevant to all grade levels can be accessed using the link http://www.nctm.org/resources/families.aspx. These resources are entitled:

• Help Your Child Succeed in Math
• Math Education Today

Parents often want to know what their child's math learning environment looks like; however, class visits aren't always an option for various reasons. The link (http://learner.org/resources/series32.html) provides classroom videos that reflect current math classrooms.

Also, a *Family Corner* located at http://www.figurethis.org/fc/family_corner.htm offers resources under categories entitled *Families and School, Families and Mathematics, Families and Homework, Families and Support, as well as Mathematics and Literature* that are quite useful for supporting your efforts to support your child.

Index

About the Author

Regina M. Mistretta, professor in The School of Education at St. John's University, received a bachelor's degree in education and mathematics from St. John's University, a master's degree in mathematics education from Brooklyn College, and a doctoral degree in mathematics education from Teachers College, Columbia University. Her nearly three decades of experience in the field of education includes teaching at elementary, middle, and high school levels, as well as at institutions of higher education. She has served as a faculty member at St. John's University for 16 years.

Mathematics education and teacher preparation are Regina's primary areas of teaching, research, and service. Her publications have appeared in journals such as *Teaching Children Mathematics, Mathematics Teaching in the Middle School, Mathematics Teacher Educator*, and *Action in Teacher Education*.

Her efforts to help bridge home and school learning environments are exemplified in her authored books entitled *Teachers Engaging Parents in Mathematical Learning: Nurturing Productive Collaboration* and *Using Teacher Inquiry for Knowing and Supporting Parents with Math*. This latest book, written directly to parents, serves to empower parents as partners in their children's mathematics education.

In addition, Regina provides professional development. To date, she has collaborated with approximately 40 pre-K–12 school learning communities encompassing teachers, administrators, and school children and their parents in the five boroughs of the metropolitan area of New York, as well as on Long Island.